THE

THEOLOGY

THE GAY THEOLOGY

by Kent Philpott

Logos International
Plainfield, N.J. 07060

All Scripture references are from the Revised Standard Version, unless otherwise indicated.

THE GAY THEOLOGY
Copyright © 1977 by Logos International
All Rights Reserved
Printed in the United States of America
Library of Congress Catalog Card Number: 77-10171
International Standard Book Number: 088270-241-6
Logos International
Plainfield, New Jersey 07061

To my co-workers in Love in Action,
and to my fellow pastors and congregation at
Church of the Open Door
in San Rafael.

Contents

Preface

This is a follow-up to *The Third Sex?* (Logos International, 1975). That book was primarily aimed at the non-Christian homosexual. This volume, however, is concerned with the homosexual who has turned to Christ and is dealing with his faith, the church, and the old nature.

Like *The Third Sex?* this book is a group effort. It is a response to needs communicated to us through the first book and our Love in Action ministry. It has been nearly four years ago that the work began and I praise God for the results I have seen and for allowing me to minister in this area. I know that the need for this outreach will grow as the homosexual population and problem grows.

Many people have contributed to this book. It takes a great deal of courage to submit to the type of interviewing that Veronica, Anne, David, and Frank experienced. They risked exposure and other possible injury in working with me on this book and I want to express to them my deepest appreciation. Dr. Robert L. Hymers, Jr., pastor of Open Door Community Church in Los Angles has been "iron on iron" with me, helping to distill my thinking and shape its content. This church has a large ministry to former homosexuals in the Hollywood, Westwood, and Santa Monica area.

The members of our church are very much behind my ministry. They have not only given me their support, but have been very generous in assisting me in the typing of the manuscript. I want to thank the church's secretary, Katie Duncan, as well as Arlene Nedrow, Becky Cain, Jadean Smith, and Nancy Hackett. They all worked overtime at their jobs and typed in the evening to help me. They are all very precious and I love them. And others have helped me in various ways. Bob, of *The Third Sex?* has allowed me to include his very excellent newsletters. Bob, one of the leaders in Love in Action, has been a great source of encouragement. Lisa Silverman has helped me on several occasions in doing paper work and some editing. Many others have played a part in the production of the book too. I especially want to thank Dan Malachuk and the Logos International staff for their courage in publishing books on homosexuality.

Kent Philpott
San Rafael, California
January, 1977

THE GAY THEOLOGY

1
Interview with Anne

KENT: Anne, would you talk about your background, how old you are, where you come from, and what you're doing now?

ANNE: I'm twenty-seven, and I'm from Portland, Oregon. I was involved in the gay life for nine years.

KENT: Tell me about your family.

ANNE: That's sort of complicated, but I lived with my father and stepmother until age twelve. Then I lived in foster homes, and at the age of sixteen I had a legal guardian.

KENT: During your early life there was confusion in the family?

ANNE: Yes.

KENT: What are you involved in now?

ANNE: Right now I work at a printing shop in the Bay Area; I'm a bindery worker. In Portland I was a secretary, but when I moved into the Bay Area, I changed occupations.

KENT: How did you get involved in homosexuality in the first place?

ANNE: Well, Kent, I'd always been attracted to women.

KENT: From about what age?

ANNE: I can remember nine to eleven years old, but mainly I got to know gay people through my brother. He is gay.

KENT: Is this an older brother?

ANNE: Yes, he's older.

KENT: You got to know other male homosexuals?

ANNE: And female homosexuals.

KENT: I see. When you were about nine or ten years old?

ANNE: No, this was when I was around seventeen or eighteen years old, but I'd always realized I was attracted to women from an early age.

KENT: Can you think of any factors that might have contributed to that?

ANNE: Probably because I was seeking a mother. At that age I wasn't attracted as much sexually as I was emotionally. I was a child yearning for a mother's affection.

KENT: Your mother didn't give you affection?

ANNE: My mother died when I was five and my father remarried when I was nine. I had a stepmother and I was taken away from my home because of child abuse. So there was no affection whatsoever from either parent.

KENT: Child abuse? Your parents abused you?

ANNE: My stepmother, yes.

KENT: Beatings you mean?

ANNE: Yes.

KENT: How about your father?

ANNE: My father was very weak and we didn't really communicate. He wasn't affectionate either. I didn't have a good relationship with him. I always considered him a very weak person and never felt comfortable with him.

KENT: Do you feel that he loved you?

ANNE: I question that. I really don't know. I don't know if he loves me or not.

KENT: How about right now?

ANNE: I haven't seen my father for quite some time, but I would say that he just doesn't care one way or the other.

KENT: Do your parents know that you were involved in homosexuality?

ANNE: My father does. I had written him many years ago asking him for help to get out of the relationship I was in. I thought I was emotionally sick and needed help. I became bitter when he never wrote back.

KENT: At this present time there's nothing going on between you and your father, or your stepmother?

ANNE: No, nothing at all.

KENT: We've identified one factor that contributed to your moving into the gay life and that is a poor relationship with your parents. At the time you didn't understand that, did you?

ANNE: No, I didn't. I didn't understand where the roots were.

KENT: What other factors contributed to your homosexuality?

ANNE: I think I viewed homosexuality as a life of excitement. I was a rebellious sort of person. I enjoyed being different and set apart and I liked being a part of a minority. I felt that I could retaliate against males, perhaps against my father. By entering into the gay life I learned more and more how to adjust to the gay life style.

KENT: You actually learned—set out to learn—how to be a part of the gay community?

ANNE: Yes, there were decisions made even then and there was the excitement of taking on lesbian affectations.

KENT: Were you butch?

ANNE: I learned to be butch. I basically was passive when I started out, but I learned, through not only sexual experience but by watching others in a group, how to act butch. I ended up locked into the butch role.

KENT: How old were you when you first had a sexual experience with a girl?

ANNE: I think the first real sexual experience was when I was about eighteen.

KENT: Prior to that time, did you have sexual fantasies about women?

ANNE: That was also progressive. When I was about twelve to fourteen it was more fantasy as far as a mother/daughter thing. But as the fantasies grew, and my experience with women grew, my fantasies became more and more sexual. I actually came out when I was eighteen. So it started with fantasies and ended up reality.

KENT: How about boys? Were you ever involved sexually with boys?

ANNE: I have been in the past.

KENT: Before your homosexuality?

ANNE: Yes.

KENT: Intercourse?

ANNE: Yes, once or twice.

KENT: What was your reaction to that?

ANNE: I would always have to be either stoned or drunk but I think I basically enjoyed it. It was the emotional problem I had with males that caused me trouble.

KENT: In other words, the sex didn't bother you but it was the men that bothered you?

ANNE: Yes.

KENT: Sounds like the bad feelings you had towards your father were being transferred to other boys.

ANNE: Yes, I can see that to a certain degree. Yet I used them as they used me, for sexual release.

KENT: Was there a time in your life when you thought, "I'm homosexual"?

ANNE: Yes, I did. I enjoyed it and was very proud of it. That was when I left for San Francisco to live with my brother. I was about eighteen when I declared myself. I was proud that I was a lesbian.

KENT: At eighteen you had your debut?

ANNE: My debut, yes.

KENT: Anne, what about experience in the gay life? Did you have lovers?

ANNE: I had a lover, but I had many affairs before actually meeting my lover. I lived with her for about five and one-half years.

KENT: With one person for about five and one-half years?

ANNE: One person, yes.

KENT: What happened to that person?

ANNE: Well, I was living with her up until I was born again. When I became a Christian I was able to leave my lover. I had tried many times before, but I always

5

went back. I left my lover and lived in an apartment by myself and started studying the Word.

KENT:How did you feel about the homosexual life when you were in it?

ANNE: I enjoyed it while I was in it. I thought it was exciting, but I was destroying myself at the same time.

KENT: What did you think about yourself? How did you feel about yourself when you were in the gay life?

ANNE: You mean my self image?

KENT: Yes.

ANNE: I would say that it was fairly bad. I don't know if it was because I was gay or not, mainly because I never felt any guilt for being gay. My self-image was fine sometimes, especially when I was using drugs.

KENT: How about God? Were you ever involved in the church? Did your parents take you to Sunday school or anything?

ANNE: No, I didn't have any church background whatsoever. At that particular time God and the church never entered my mind.

KENT: Did you ever talk about God, the church, the Bible when you were involved in homosexuality?

ANNE: No. No way!

KENT: Just totally left out?

ANNE: Totally left out.

KENT: How is it that you became a Christian?

ANNE: Up until about three months before I was born again I started delving into the occult and studying Carlos Castenada. I realized there was something supernatural happening, but was not quite sure what it was. During that time a gay friend of mine, a male friend as a matter of fact, called me. He had recently moved into the area and said he was having a spiritual breakthrough. A few weeks later I got together with him and he told me about Jesus. Shortly after, I accepted the Lord.

KENT: This happened in a fairly short space of time?

ANNE: Yes.

KENT: What did you think about homosexuality after you had become a Christian?

ANNE: I think for the most part I looked at my gay life and realized how destructive it had been on my own person and the people around me. I saw what a lie it was. It was like being able to see for the first time. I realized how locked in I had been to a particular life style without seeing any other perspective. I saw how it involved my whole soul and person.

KENT: You said that when you became a Christian you were living with a woman?

ANNE: Yes, that's right.

KENT: How did she relate to your Christianity?

ANNE: With a great deal of violence, physical violence as a matter of fact.

KENT: Were you in the butch role in this relationship?

ANNE: I was butch in bed, but she was more aggressive in life. She was stronger than I. We had delved into a lot of violence in our relationship. It didn't begin that way but it ended up in a very violent type of relationship. When I moved out she came over and ripped my apartment apart. She hated the idea that I was a Christian.

KENT: Did you feel like leaving Christ then?

ANNE: No. It was tremendous in a way. Though that experience took place with such violence, the Lord was there and gave me great strength and power. After that there was no way they could prove that the Lord was not in my life.

KENT: What happened then? Did you think about becoming a part of a church?

ANNE: At that particular point I was more into the Word. Yes, I wanted fellowship but I had problems because of the gay background.

KENT: You felt you wouldn't be accepted?

ANNE: Yes. I would speak of my struggles as being drug-related. I was never able to talk about the real problems, which were my temptations to continue involvement in the homosexual world.

KENT: What was your first introduction to a church?

ANNE: I think my first introduction to a church was through the gay friend whom I mentioned before. His family suggested that I go to a church. I looked around and found one. I believe God led me into a church that I would feel comfortable in.

KENT: Can you share some of your feelings concerning what was happening to you at that early stage in your Christian life, particularly as related to problems you experienced?

ANNE: At that particular point I never thought I would be tempted after I was born again.

KENT: You thought that Jesus was going to take it all away?

ANNE: Yes, every bit of it. But I was mistaken. Now I know that there are going to be times of temptation. But I think the biggest problem was interacting with the rest of the church without being honest about my struggles, always having to cover it up. I would have to say I was having struggles because of drugs, and I wasn't really being honest. I think that was the biggest frustration I had.

8

KENT: This is what I wanted to get to, these sort of things. Try to be more specific.

ANNE: Okay. Up until the first couple of years after I was born again, I was very fearful about mentioning anything about homosexuality. When temptations came up, I'd always talked about them as being related to drugs. But at one point I got feeling so much alone in my struggles that I ended up blurting out the fact that I was a homosexual to two of my friends.

KENT: Girl friends?

ANNE: One guy and one girl. I almost expected them, because of past experience, to reject me. It was almost like seeing if grace was for real.

KENT: So what happened?

ANNE: They accepted me beautifully. As a matter of fact, the girl had had struggles herself with that and the other man had past experiences.

KENT: To your surprise you didn't get rejected.

ANNE: I didn't get rejected and yet I was not used to having them open up. They were fearful, just as I was all this time.

KENT: You gradually began to become a part of the fellowship in the church?

ANNE: Yes, I did.

KENT: What effect did that have on you?

ANNE: Well, at first it was difficult. Again I'll say that my biggest temptation was to set myself apart and not interact with the church. I used my gay background as an excuse. I wanted to make myself a recluse and not get involved. But God has progressively shown me that everybody has struggles. He will lead the people into your life that you are able to talk to. He doesn't want us to be set apart.

KENT: Does the church know you have a gay background?

ANNE: No. A few people do; of course, the pastors do.

KENT: You told the pastors?

ANNE: Oh, yes.

KENT: How soon after your conversion?

ANNE: About two years after my conversion.

KENT: How long ago was it that you became a Christian, Anne?

ANNE: About three years.

KENT: What did they say to you when you told them?

ANNE: They were surprised but so accepting, and they've been so much help ever since. They said that other people involved in the church have gay backgrounds and are sharing the same sort of struggles that I did. They are very willing to help in whatever area I need.

KENT: I wish that would be the experience of everyone who's moving from gay to Christ. Do you know that everyone does not have that experience in a church?

ANNE: Yes, I also have experienced a few rejections here and there from different people, but for the most part the congregation has been very willing to accept me.

KENT: Many times it's not rejection you're receiving so much as it is a fear reaction, homophobia even, because many people are insecure about their own sexual identities. How did you deal with your temptations? You mentioned that you thought the temptations would go away but they didn't. What did you do about them?

ANNE: About my temptations? I sought help through

a church counselor and that helped me a great deal. I started realizing that temptation is normal. I thought God had taken it all away so I found a great deal of comfort in knowing that I will be tempted. But God is there to give me strength to endure it. And I'm also learning through temptations about grace, which I think is very important.

KENT: The early part of your Christian life was marked by loneliness?

ANNE: It was aloneness but not loneliness. Christ was so much a part of me that He enabled me to not only leave my lover but to leave the society and all the people that I was involved with.

KENT: What did your gay friends do about your conversion? How did they relate to you?

ANNE: There was persecution. I mean they laughed at me and thought that I was on another "trip."

KENT: Had you been involved in the bar scene to any extent?

ANNE: Very much so.

KENT: You lost a whole social life then, didn't you?

ANNE: Oh, completely. All the people I knew were homosexuals. There was maybe one straight person but he wasn't a friend, just an acquaintance. I was involved in the whole culture.

KENT: You had cultural shock? They laughed at you and thought you were crazy?

ANNE: They thought I was crazy. And it seemed to me that after I was born again, people who had never been interested before were sexually interested in me. I thought that was a little strange.

KENT: I hear that so much, Anne, so much. Just at the point of conversion sex comes into your life that you

11

never thought was going to come around. Any further thoughts along the line of what you experienced from your gay friends?

ANNE: Not really. I think the basic thing was persecution.

KENT: Did it stop?

ANNE: No, not until I moved out of the area.

KENT: You left the immediate area?

ANNE: Yes, and moved to a different city.

KENT: What if you'd stayed there? Do you think you might have fallen back into it?

ANNE: I think not, because my gay experience was destructive to me. I saw it, after being born again, for what it really was.

KENT: But at one time you thought it was beautiful?

ANNE: During the time, yes. But then, after you're born again, you see things completely different.

KENT: How did you deal with your sexual drive after your conversion? Did your sexual drive go away?

ANNE: Oh, no! It's still alive. I think that for the most part I was so involved with learning the Word and with Christ that sex became secondary. I got into masturbation for a while and I realized it only led to further frustration. I dealt with it by praying and trying to keep it under control.

KENT: That helped with the fantasies?

ANNE: Yes.

KENT: Have you, in the several years that you've been a Christian, ever gone back into the gay life?

ANNE: No, I can't say that I have. I fooled around with one individual, but not to the point of a sexual experience.

KENT: Can you isolate any factors that might have

contributed to that? How did you get to that point?

ANNE: I think the main factor was thinking I was never going to be tempted again, so I felt safe in entering into an emotional relationship with this person.

KENT: Was it with another Christian girl?

ANNE: She was born again soon after. We had a very strong emotional relationship but then ended up desiring each other physically. We were both so very startled and concerned about the heavy temptation that we sought counsel.

KENT: You did the right thing. People coming out of the gay life have to realize that they are vulnerable and that most of the time temptation starts off in a very intimate emotional way. We can't close ourselves off though, don't you agree, Anne?

ANNE: No. I think that's very unhealthy. I think it is a big temptation, though, to a lot of people who have experienced gay life. We often fear any emotional involvement because of its potential for ending in a sexual thing.

KENT: Sex ruins friendships, doesn't it?

ANNE: It certainly does.

KENT: Anne, are you attracted to women now?

ANNE: A sexual attraction? No. For the most part, no. I'm still emotionally very attracted to women.

KENT: What happened to all those sexual feelings?

ANNE: Before I was born again, I was sexually very active and was attracted to many, many types of women. Once I was born again I lost the attraction to women. I gained an attraction to men but still struggled like heck relating emotionally to men. Now I'm attracted to men, but all these problems have to be

13

worked out as far as relating to men in an emotional way.

KENT: You have difficulty relating to men on an emotional level? Can you shed some light on that?

ANNE: I think it is the fear of rejection. I think that my fear of rejection would stop even any pursuit of an involvement with a man. It's almost a safeguard for me rather than being rejected by him. I would keep a distance from him, not allowing him to get close enough to do that. Also, I have a lot of resentment for males and that has to be worked out.

KENT: The resentment goes back to your father perhaps?

ANNE: I think that's one of the possibilities. I'm not afraid of the male sexually so I think it would probably be being vulnerable or hurt. Rejection, I think.

KENT: Do you feel that you are attractive to men?

ANNE: I'm beginning to feel more and more that I am attractive to men.

KENT: Do you think that a man would keep his distance from you if he found that you had been gay?

ANNE: I think many men would, yes.

KENT: If you became emotionally involved with a man, do you think you would divulge your background?

ANNE: I think I would almost have to if I wanted an honest relationship if only because that background did exist for many years. There are a lot of things that would have to be worked out and I'm sure he would see it and wonder why. So I would want to be able to express that to him.

KENT: It's not that you don't desire a man sexually but you're afraid of the rejection. Anne, now let me be plain. You feel that if a person knew your background he would reject you?

ANNE: No, I think it goes deeper than that. If they got to know me maybe they wouldn't like me as a person and then reject me. I'm not sure.

KENT: You felt confidence in your being attractive to women but you doubt that with men?

ANNE: Yes, I felt much safer with women than men. I was more confident in myself.

KENT: That's very true in the homosexual community. There is considerable tension in the heterosexual interpersonal boy/girl kind of relationship. In heterosexual relations there is a greater threat of rejection, isn't there? There's more possibility of being hurt. Sex is more free wheeling and less subject to anxiety in the homosexual community.

ANNE: Oh, yes!

KENT: Do you think that there will be a possibility of your being married some day?

ANNE: I think there's a possibility of that. My desires right now do not lie along that line, but I'm certainly open for it.

KENT: Do you consider yourself homosexual or heterosexual?

ANNE: I consider myself heterosexual.

KENT: Can you give more content to that, Anne? Why do you feel you're heterosexual?

ANNE: Mainly because I have lost so much of the attraction I had for women and I desire to be free from the emotional problems I have with men. I desire men. I enjoy responding to men but I know that there are so many things that have to be worked out. I believe the Lord will do it in His time. The main thing is I am

15

enjoying myself as a woman, not as a homosexual. It is a pleasing experience for me for the first time.

KENT: There is the possibility of marriage but you're not there yet.

ANNE: No, I'm not there yet.

KENT: You have talked to gay male friends and haven't they expressed sort of the same kinds of fears of rejection from women?

ANNE: Yes, they have. In fact, I know quite a few have experienced the same thing. I think they express it as fear and rejection or some resentment, but it's all basically the same thing.

KENT: We're kind of the same, aren't we?

ANNE: Yeah, we sure are.

KENT: People are people. One of the things you expressed is that you are prone to isolate yourself. Can you tell me more about that?

ANNE: I'll say that the biggest temptation I have is to use the excuse of having a homosexual background to set my self apart and isolate myself from interacting with other people, especially in the church. I know the Bible says not to forsake the gathering of ourselves together. God knows what He's talking about. I found that when I did that I would slip back into old habits and into old life style patterns.

KENT: I can say that you're an attractive person and would be very acceptable in any men's set. How do you feel about that?

ANNE: Well, Kent, the first thing that comes to mind is that I was not this way a few years ago. Right after I was born again I still had lesbian affectations and mannerisms.

KENT: What did you do about the affectations?

16

ANNE: I can't say I did much of anything. It was a process that God took me through. I found myself intentionally gaining weight for safety, trying to be as unattractive as I could to the opposite sex so I wouldn't have to cope with those problems. Within the last year God has gotten my weight under control and my desire to be attractive has grown. I was not always attractive to men, nor to myself, so it's a matter of self-image that has changed for me.

KENT: This all says metamorphosis to me.

ANNE: That's sort of what it is.

KENT: It really does. You're involved in change. Your whole life is opening up. Let's talk about some of the particular problems you experienced in relating to people in the church.

ANNE: Okay. Well again, the greatest problem was thinking that I was alone with my struggles, that I was the only person in the Christian circle with a gay background. It's funny because I almost felt like I was having to live a lie again. I became very frustrated thinking I was all alone, until I found out there are many, many people with gay backgrounds who felt just like I did. Now they are beginning to come together.

KENT: What about the present? What are you feeling now and what are you doing?

ANNE: Again, the biggest thing that's coming about in a personal way is the fact that I'm enjoying being a woman. I'm enjoying getting to know men. It's a slow process, but I'm starting to do that as well as getting to know different people with gay backgrounds, without gay backgrounds. I'm finding out that we're all basically the same. One of the important things to remember is that it's a process. The Christian walk is a process. The changes come about in time just as it was when we learned how to be gay. I think if we keep remembering that we won't so easily get distressed and frustrated. It's continual. It's reeducating yourself, it's relearning habits. God will change you, but you have to desire that change too.

KENT: You're still working in the printing job?

ANNE: Yes, I am.

KENT: And you're active in your church?

ANNE: Yes.

KENT: Are you involved in any ministries right now?

ANNE: I'm involved. My prayers and concerns right now are for an outreach to gays for my church. They're thrilled about it, so my immediate plans for the future and vision that I have is to become more and more active in this new ministry.

KENT: You want to begin reaching out to other people with a gay background?

ANNE: Yes. That's my heart's desire right now.

KENT: Can you tell me some of the things that helped you over the rough spots? You've had rough spots, Anne?

ANNE: Oh, yes! Many—many. I would say what helped me over the rough spots was remembering what God had done in the past. But then I think that God doesn't work as fast as He should in my life.

KENT: You're a little impatient with God?

ANNE: Yes! But then I look back on the different areas; He's been faithful, gentle and patient. I don't think He's ever going to fail me, so that's what basically helps me over rough spots.

KENT: What kind of devotional life do you have?

ANNE: Devotional life— do you mean Bible reading?

Well, I'm usually up in the morning—my mornings are my favorite time— about five.

KENT: That's early.

ANNE: Oh, I love it! I love it. I go to sleep very early at night but I'm up at five or earlier and I spend a few hours in prayer and in the Word. That starts my day off fantastically.

KENT: That beats me, Anne. I'll tell you, that beats me. So you have a strong devotional life and you're part of a church membership? Do you tithe your money to that church?

ANNE: I give ten percent to the church and also to people I come in contact with that the Lord leads me to give to.

KENT: You're being faithful over the regular things. That's important. Anything else that helps when you're facing difficulties?

ANNE: I think that the worst thing you can do is isolate yourself and be self-indulgent. We need to find a few people we can talk with and share burdens with. I think there's a healing process involved in fellowship with other Christians. I find that friends are very helpful to me, but it's mainly the Lord. It's mainly the Lord.

2
Interview
with Brother Frank

Frank, known to many as "Brother" Frank is a leader in Love in Action. He has prepared numerous tapes including, "Pitfalls," "Introduction to Love in Action," and "How to Counsel a Homosexual."

KENT: Frank, would you relate briefly some of your background, as much as you feel you would like to share?

FRANK: I am forty-seven years old. I've been a Christian for a long time, most of my life. I fell away from the Lord when I was about twenty. I received the Lord when I was thirteen and for about seven years I followed the Lord quite seriously.

KENT: You tried to be a serious Christian?

FRANK: Yes. I was very serious about following the Lord. This was, of course, quite a few years ago. The charismatic movement was not around at that time. We had no knowledge of the Holy Spirit, and so forth, to guide us. So it was rather a flat type of religious experience. I did love the Lord. When I reached twenty I had to make a decision between my sexual life and my Christian life.

KENT: At that time were you conscious of being different, of being homosexual?

FRANK: I can remember being sort of homosexual-oriented back to about three years old, playing with the neighborhood kids and so forth. But I really didn't know the word or think I was different than anybody else until I was probably around twelve or thirteen years old. And then I began to realize that maybe things weren't quite right. It was at that time that I became saved. I had a homosexual minister. He assured me everything was okay and that following a homosexual life, although different than other people, was the right way to go for me. I remember him saying that homosexuality was a beautiful thing and that many people in literature were homosexual, and, according to him, many people in the Bible had homosexual relationships. So he guided me along this path and I didn't feel as outcast as before.

KENT: Do you feel that if your minister had said homosexuality was wrong and had given you some counsel and help, you might have gotten over it?

FRANK: Sure I would. I am positive. I would not have been homosexual. But he painted a very beautiful picture of homosexuality. When I graduated from high school I left that town and went to San Francisco. I was organist in various churches. The message wasn't the same. Homosexuality in these churches wasn't a very beautiful, wonderful life style. It was strict condemnation, of course; they condemned the person

21

along with the act. Homosexuality was totally taboo. For the first time in my life I began to have conflicts. Maybe my minister hadn't been right. I had never truly believed that he was right, but I wanted to believe that he was. It was the easier path for me. It made life a lot easier. And then, when I went to another church and found that they had an entirely different idea about the subject, it brought conflict into my life. Being gay was so engrained in me by that time that I spent a couple of very difficult years. Finally I dropped the church. I was through with the church at about twenty-two.

KENT: Is it at that point that you began to commit yourself to a homosexual life style?

FRANK: Right, and I was! Those two years between twenty and twenty-two were very difficult for me. I was nervous and it affected my music and everything. After I dropped the church I settled back and the nervousness left.

KENT: The conflict produced a situation where you didn't want to be around Christian people?

FRANK: Right.

KENT: Were you rejecting Christ as well?

FRANK: No, not really. I was rejecting the church. I got very angry at the church. When anyone mentioned church to me I got upset. Anytime there was anything on the ballot to make churches pay taxes, I was for it. I was really dead set against the church. I was mad. They had rejected me along with homosexuality. They hadn't reached down to me in any loving way. It was just total rejection. I didn't want any part of it and anything bad that happened to the church, I was happy about it.

KENT: This situation where you were actually a

Christian, but rejected the church, persisted for about twenty years?

FRANK: Yes, I was forty-three when I came back to the Lord.

KENT: Frank, what touched you? What were the factors that brought you back into a fuller relationship with Christ and the Church?

FRANK: Of course, reaching forty is a very difficult period in anyone's life. When I turned forty, I reevaluated my life. It was very unsatisfactory and I was very unhappy. As I looked back, it hadn't been beautiful as my minister told me it would be. It was a sordid life. As you get older, anything good about homosexuality passes away and you are left with all of the bad things. You no longer are attractive and you cannot make contact with any people. You have to pay for any sex you get. And then there is no involvement, there is no love. No friendship is involved; just a business transaction. So the rejection of the homosexual life is very intense. I knew that life was not good and I was doing things that I would not have done before.

KENT: This reflection brought you to a place of re-examination?

FRANK: It brought me to a searching place.

KENT: You were wondering what the truth was all over again?

FRANK: But, you know, it was hopeless. I had already tried the church and I knew that they had rejected me. I didn't even think of trying the church again. I knew my life was out of order, but the church didn't seem like the answer at that time. Then two years later, a very fine Christian young man came into my life. I watched him grow in the Lord. In fact, I knew him

23

before he was saved and I saw the change in his life. I also saw the workings of the Holy Spirit. My church had believed all of the gifts died with the last apostle and I had always believed this, but my young friend was a charismatic Christian. He seemed so happy and I had seen his life change so dramatically. For about a year his life troubled me. I saw the contrast between his happy, joyful life and my miserable life. It was not what he said to me, but it was his day-by-day actions. It was what he *was* rather than what he *said* that brought me back to the Lord. And so I came to a moment of decision. I was on my way to a very disreputable house of sin, for the first time, and it was a new lower experience for me. I was leaving my office when the Lord "touched me" and gave me sort of an ultimatum. If I was going to do this, I felt God was saying to me that He would not protect me as He had my whole life. This time I was going to walk away from Him if I went into this additional sin. It was at that moment I had to make the decision. Right at that point I asked my friend, who was working with me, to take me to his church. He was very surprised. He didn't think it was possible for me to be saved. He thought I was totally hopeless, and, I must admit, I had given him a pretty bad time. I had really tested that boy and so he was probably the most surprised person on earth when I asked him to take me to his church. But he did. We left immediately. He was very knowledgeable of the Lord. He said this prayer and had me repeat it after him. It was a great time for me. It was a time of my burden being lifted. It worked! The Lord came into my life at that time.

KENT: How many years ago was that?

FRANK: It was nearly four years ago now.

KENT: At that point, you began to become concerned about the ministry to people in the homosexual life.

FRANK: Well, yes. Not that particular day. Immediately I thought I was relieved from the homosexual life. I wanted out. I felt I was out of the homosexual life. I mean, it is just such a simple thing to say that sinner's prayer, but it changed my life. But then, there I was in a church and very unsure because I didn't know if they would accept me or not. I was very cautious and didn't tell anyone about my homosexuality.

KENT: You kept your past secret?

FRANK: Yes. And I had a tough time because I couldn't share with anyone.

KENT: Could you be specific? What was the problem; why was it you felt you had a bad time?

FRANK: I didn't relate to the standard family situation. Most of the people in the church are married with little children and I felt that if they knew about me they would grab their children and run. I just felt out of place. But I tried my best to work into the fellowship. They were different from my other church. They were a very loving group of people and they did accept me. As time went by I felt their love and acceptance. I thought I could share with them a little bit. I began sharing with the boy that brought me to the Lord.

KENT: You told him about your background?

FRANK: Yes, I did.

KENT: How did he react to you?

FRANK: He knew it all the time so it came as no surprise, but I didn't know he knew. So I found I could talk to him.

KENT: That meant a lot to be able to talk to somebody.

FRANK: Yes, it did. For the first few months of my new salvation I couldn't talk to anyone. I was really bottled up inside. I was unsure of what I had done—joining the church again.

KENT: You were feeling that it was going to fall out from underneath you once more?

FRANK: Yes. I thought maybe it would be a repeat of what I had been through before.

KENT: Were there problems in the church?

FRANK: Yes, there were.

KENT: It wasn't smooth and easygoing for you?

FRANK: It wasn't that easy, but they were a loving group of people and I saw they were different. They weren't Sunday Christians. They were every-day-of-the-week Christians. They would come visit me during the week and ask how I was doing. They were concerned! It was quite different, and I had hopes that it would work.

KENT: Let me ask you a very common question, Frank. After your conversion, or after your renewal, did you have any temptations? Were you still struggling with homosexuality?

FRANK: The answer is that the Lord carried me in His hands for about six or eight months. However, Satan brought all sorts of tempting situations to me. Everything that was totally unavailable to me before became available.

KENT: You mean it was easy sex all of a sudden?

FRANK: Easy sex with beautiful young people. Things that I could never have had, Satan brought to me. But the Lord strengthened me. I turned down

26

things that I would have never before turned down and I couldn't believe that I actually said no. I heard myself saying no and it didn't seem like me. It was such an entirely different situation.

KENT: I remember you telling me about picking up a hitchhiker once.

FRANK: Yes, I picked up a hitchhiker, a fine-looking young man, who wanted me to go home with him. I told him that all I could talk to him about was Jesus Christ if I did go home with him. So the Lord carried me in His hands for about eight months. He gave me time to get strong in His Word. He gave me time to get into full fellowship with my church.

KENT: You had the experience of being carried by God; then after a period of time, about eight months, you began to face the old temptation.

FRANK: Yes.

KENT: You had to deal with homosexuality again?

FRANK: I did have to deal with it. God said He would always give us a way out. During that eight months I spent a lot of time in the Scripture. I wanted to make this work and I made a real effort to make it work. I attended midweek services, and so forth. I fellowshiped with my friends in the church.

KENT: You were not what might be considered a casual church goer?

FRANK: That's right and I made every effort possible. And the young man who brought me back to the Lord was a real help. He admonished me and was kind of my spiritual leader. I think the Holy Spirit gave him what to say to me and how to guide me. He was very competent in his guidance. By the time the Lord set me down and expected me to operate on my level I was pretty prepared for it. I had a lot of tempting situations, and it was harder to say no now.

KENT: Now that you were on your own, it was a little harder to say no?

FRANK: Yes. And after I would turn something down, I would think about it. I would think, "Gee, I wish that I had said yes," and I had second thoughts. It was hard to bring my mind and imagination into obedience to the Lord. It took some work to do that.

KENT: How about fantasies, Frank? Did you have a problem with them?

FRANK: I have never had the problem that many people go through with fantasies. I have had some and still do sometimes but they are not an important thing in my life. I just do something else when I get them. I go to prayer, I go to something else. Or I simply ask the Lord to take them away.

KENT: That is an important factor here. Could you describe one or two principles that were helpful to you?

FRANK: I had seen the low degradation of the homosexual life and I didn't want to go back. It wasn't alluring. It wasn't like I was naive and still thought it was glamorous. I mean, as you get older, you get a little wiser and although situations were tempting, going back to that life style wasn't tempting. I didn't want to return to that life style and I knew that if I did fall, that might take me back to it. I knew the despair of it all. I knew how difficult it would be to get back to the Lord again.

KENT: I have heard you talk about honesty. When I hear you saying this, I know that you are being honest. You weren't able to cover over the sex with a cloak of glamour, beauty and pleasure. You were honest enough to see what it really was.

FRANK: Yes, we do have to be honest with ourselves and it is very difficult. One of the things we learn in the Bible is that Jesus is called the Truth, and the Truth sets us free. There are lots of Scriptures like that. I didn't know if God would take me back a third time, and I thought, "This has got to work." I made every effort to be honest with God and myself. I knew that a few moments of pleasure could separate me from the Lord. I felt that the lines were drawn and this time I had to make a go of it.

KENT: Frank, let me ask you about the people you had been involved with, for example, lovers and gay friends.

FRANK: Oh, this is very interesting, really. I had a lover up until the day I was saved. He was supposed to come over the next day. I didn't live with him. I wasn't intending to have relations with him, I was simply going to tell him that I accepted Christ. I told him to come over. I thought he would show up but he didn't. He had been my lover and friend for eleven years, though I had never lived with him. He didn't show up and it was six months before he called me.

KENT: Six months?

FRANK: Yes. I had seen him every week, just all of the time before then. And when he finally called he said there was something in my voice that told him to stay away. Just the tone of voice. He knew me quite well, of course, and something in my voice had said "stay away." This was apparently God working in my life. The Lord knew that I wouldn't be able to handle this temptation and He simply kept him away from me.

29

KENT: It wasn't a conscious choice on your part to separate yourself. You wanted to communicate Christ to him, but God did it for you.

FRANK: I wasn't strong enough to face the situation. It is incredible that he would disappear for six months!

KENT: Let's put this in a different perspective. If you had been able to counsel yourself, would you have advised staying away from the former lover or attempting to help him?

FRANK: I think a new Christian has to stay away. I think God did the right thing in my life. Your friends and close associates can be quite persuasive. In fact, I had other relationships besides this one and these people attacked me and wanted me back into the gay life. People can be very persuasive and I think it is necessary to avoid them for a while until you build up your strength in the Lord. When my lover did come back, after six months, I was strong and could talk to him freely. I certainly think old friends can be damaging to you.

KENT: Frank, is there anything else you want to say about gay friends?

FRANK: For one thing, I did have gay friends. I mean, everyone does have friends. Of course, they simply could not accept me following the Lord. They couldn't accept it and many of them would phone me. I would tell them what was happening in my life and usually that was the last phone call I ever received from them. The funny thing about it is that when I had Jesus Christ in my life, I didn't need them any longer. I had a new group of people. I had my church. I grew to really love the people in my church. The people that had previously been my friends were not as important to me as they once were. I didn't value their opinions any longer. I would have liked to have brought them to the Lord, but it seemed as if that was impossible. They did not relate at all to my new life, to my new birth. So they just fell away.

KENT: How did you feel about them?

FRANK: I wasn't sad about it. I really wasn't. I was happy to see them go. I knew they were a source of trouble in my life. So I made a point of telling them what had happened.

KENT: That is a very good point. I'm glad you said that.

FRANK: Once I told them, that was the end of it. I never saw them again, most of them. It eliminated a lot of problems in my life.

KENT: Did it leave you feeling empty?

FRANK: No, it didn't because my fellowship was so great in the church.

KENT: You put a lot of emphasis on your church.

FRANK: Right.

KENT: Of all the things that I have heard you say here, this is the key. It is the fellowship.

FRANK: I don't know how anyone could follow the Lord and not be in fellowship. I think that it would be terribly difficult.

KENT: Now, I hear so many people say that they fear rejection from the Christian community. Did you experience any of that at all?

FRANK: No. There was no rejection from my fellowship. I thought there would be.

KENT: We have been involved in ministering to

ex-gays for several years now. We know that many people do get rejected.

FRANK: Yes, they do. I mean lots of churches do. Lots of churches don't understand. They throw out the person with the sin. And that's exactly what happened to me in my earlier life. That is part of our ministry, to help churches understand and accept homosexuals who want out of that trap.

KENT: That is one of the things we are seeking to do.

FRANK: It is their responsibility to accept the ex-homosexual into the mainstream of their fellowship. That is what our church did. They accepted me right into mainstream of their fellowship. I was not a second-class citizen or a second-class Christian.

KENT: And you became the organist there, didn't you?

FRANK: Yes. I became the church organist. And everyone in my church now knows that I was homosexual.

KENT: Would you counsel all ex-gays to tell their church?

FRANK: I think they have to tell their pastor. It is very important to tell their pastor.

KENT: At least the pastor?

FRANK: I don't think it is particularly anyone's business in the church what a person was before he came to the Lord, but because of witnessing and other things, we do have to tell. I mean, if it is going to help, then we do have to use our past to help the Lord.

KENT: What I am hearing is that sometimes it is okay for someone to tell their whole church, sometimes not. It is up to their own discretion. But they should tell their pastor?

FRANK: They should tell their pastor. I think it is absolutely essential that they do that.

KENT: Why?

FRANK: So that they at least have someone they can share with. They have got to share with someone and a pastor should know. Then your testimony could be used to help another person in a similar situation. The threat of exposure would be reduced, too.

KENT: Thank you, Frank. That was particularly helpful. Now, could you zero in on any particular problems you have faced the last four years of your Christian life?

FRANK: Right after I got saved I had to be secretive about what I had been. I made that problem for myself. I found I could have shared everything with my fellowship, but I didn't. I was worrying about what they would think of me, and rejection and so forth. However, the problem did not exist. That was a problem of my own making. Also, I had to turn down sexual situations, which have been difficult to do. Other than that, we all have peaks and valleys. We all have times when He doesn't seem so close. But this is not a problem only homosexuals go through. This is a problem that all Christians experience. That is one thing that I have found, that there aren't any problems strictly peculiar to the ex-homosexual. Homosexuals often are filled with self-pity because they are denied their sexual outlet. They do not realize that there are many single Christians who don't have any sexual outlet either.

KENT: Frank, did you ever get mad at God? Did you feel you were discriminated against?

FRANK: Sure you can feel that way if you don't think it

through. If you are determined to be in a self-pity mood, you can get mad at God. You begin to think that the pressures are too great and that He is asking too much of you. But if you look around, you find that people in your fellowship are in the prime of their lives and still single for various reasons. They are not homosexual but they still have this same problem. We tend to think the problems are homosexual problems when they aren't. They are problems common to all Christians.

KENT: When you were renewed in the Lord, did you become heterosexual?

FRANK: No, I became a new creation in Christ. I still had the temptations that any homosexual has.

KENT: Did you think that coming back to the Lord might change your sexual preference?

FRANK: No, I didn't have the idea that I would automatically become heterosexual. All I knew is that I didn't like the homosexual life style and I wanted out of it. I just thought of myself as a new creature in Christ, naturally part of the family of God. I was no longer a homosexual, but I did not consider myself heterosexual. Women still did not appeal to me.

KENT: How about now?

FRANK: Yes, now is quite a different story. This is after four years of continual fellowship in the Lord.

KENT: Fellowship is the key.

FRANK: I think it was fellowship. I have been able to relate so well to the women in my church. They are very loving and kind women, women you can honor. I have an entirely different view of women now. Marriage is a distinct possibility in my life right now, although I wouldn't rush into it. It is a definite possibility. It is something I have considered.

KENT: Would you be content if you never married?

FRANK: Yes, I am content in the Lord. And if I stay single the rest of my life, this is just fine with me. I'm happy the way I am. I don't need a wife, though I might like to have one.

KENT: You are not on a mad search for a woman?

FRANK: No, I'm not on a search for a woman. I do know about a dozen married people who were formerly homosexual. And they are very, very happy. Sometimes I look at their happiness and wish that I had that, and I know it is possible. They almost seem to have a better relationship than normal straight relationships because the Lord has brought them women who are His gift. So that is why I am now not seeking or trying to find a wife under my own power. If the Lord brought one to me I would be glad and very thankful. I look to the Lord for all of my needs. And I am seeking Him first and He adds what He wants to in my life.

KENT: Are you a moody person, Frank?

FRANK: Do you think I am?

KENT: You seem to be on a pretty even keel. What I am trying to get at is after being with the Lord for four years, do you experience spiritual moods, where you are up and down?

FRANK: Yes, I do. I have times when I am up and times when I am down.

KENT: Have you ever felt like you wanted to leave Christ and go back into the gay life?

FRANK: Not seriously. Like I said earlier, we do have wilderness experiences where we feel lost and far away from the Lord. Of course, the enemy will tell you you should go back to something that you know better than

35

this, or that, since you have been a homosexual all of your life, you made a mistake to leave it. Common sense told me that I now have a better life. I look back over the last four years in which I have been happy and there has been no reason for me to go back to the old life.

KENT: I know one of the elements in that happiness is that you are involved in actual ministry.

FRANK: Right.

KENT: Tell about the ministry and what it means to you.

FRANK: The ministry came about because I knew how difficult it was for homosexuals who came to Jesus to share with anyone about their past. So I knew there was a need for an outreach to homosexuals. It was vital, I knew, to be able to share openly and not have to hide things. We got together a fellowship of ex-homosexuals, Christians who had been homo-sexual, so they could unburden themselves and not have to live with tension in their lives.

KENT: Have you benefited from that ministry yourself?

FRANK: Yes. You know, the Lord's love cannot be bottled within us. It has to be passed on and you benefit from it. The Lord fills me with His love and expects it to go out from me to others. This outreach has been a wonderful factor in my life and has helped keep me on a good spiritual plane. It has gotten me through some rough spots.

KENT: It is good you mentioned rough spots. It's an ongoing flow of following Jesus on a day-by-day basis and ministering that meets those needs.

FRANK: Anyone who is having problems with their

Christian walk may need to be reaching out to other people.

KENT: As you look toward your future, Frank, what about that?

FRANK: I don't know what the future holds. I want to be as submissive to the Lord as I can be. I want to do what He wants me to do. Next year perhaps my involvement with Love in Action will grow. I don't know what He has in mind for me except that the ministry is growing quite rapidly. There is much correspondence. There are many tapes to send out. There are a lot of people who are having troubles in their lives.

KENT: I see there is purpose in your life.

FRANK: Yes, I do have a purpose. Life is not meaningless. So many people go through life without having a purpose. They do not know why they are here or why they exist. That is not the case for me. I love the Lord and He fills my soul and has given me a purpose—something to do.

KENT: I wish all of the people who come out of the gay life would experience that as well. We both know that it is not as easy as that sometimes, but the possibility is there.

FRANK: Everyone can reach out to another person. It may be difficult. They may not know how to go about it, but if they just talk to the Lord about it, He always provides a way. God never asks anything that He doesn't enable us to do.

KENT: Frank, thanks for sharing these things.

3
Interview
with Veronica

KENT: To begin with would you tell me a bit about yourself. Include such things as your age, where you are from, just any kind of background material.

VERONICA: I am thirty-four years old. I was born in Melbourne, Australia in 1942 and presently I am living in Toronto, Canada. I immigrated when I was twenty-three.

KENT: You are living in Toronto. How long have you been there?

VERONICA: I have been in Toronto for the last eight years.

KENT: What kind of work do you do?

VERONICA: I am a registered nurse.

KENT: How long have you been doing that kind of work?

VERONICA: Since I was seventeen years old.

KENT: A long time.

VERONICA: Yes, a long time. It is my whole life.

KENT: Do you like it?

VERONICA: Yes, I love it. I love the caring ministry you have in nursing.

KENT: Tell me please about how you became involved in homosexuality?

VERONICA: I wasn't really aware of the direction my sexuality was taking. When I was seventeen I was a very naive person. I have explained to you already about the relationship that was initiated when I was a little girl.

KENT: Would you tell me more about that please?

VERONICA: When I was six years old my parents were divorced and the family was split up. There were three of us; I was the youngest. There was about six years between my sister and myself. My mother was a very pretty lady. My father was in the war and was away a lot. The men in my life were my mother's lovers. There was no real male figure in my life at that time except for my brother, who is ten years older than I am. When my father found out about my mother's infidelity he was deeply hurt. He wasn't capable of deciding on the future of the family and let his parents decide what was best for us. My brother and my sister were raised by my grandparents, and I was shipped off to an aunt and uncle who had no children and were in their forties. I was six years old at this time. I can't remember what happened to initiate the sexuality between my uncle and myself.

KENT: You were living with your uncle and he molested you?

VERONICA: As I said, I can't remember how it happened. I know that it wasn't a full sexual expression at that time, because I was too small.

KENT: Fondling?

VERONICA: Yes, fondling and a clitoral type of thing. As I got older he would try (it is quite painful, you know, Kent, to bring this up again) to force an entry and he would think of all sorts of things to accomplish this. I really didn't realize what was going on.

KENT: You were almost trapped. And there was no way of getting out of it?

VERONICA: Yes, and I was warned to be quiet. And, being young and small, I listened to what he said. I didn't tell anyone. I was afraid of him.

KENT: Veronica, I'm hearing that there was gradual fear and mistrust of men beginning to develop in you.

VERONICA: Yes, right there. I have no feelings of love for my uncle. He was a very domineering person and could be violent. I was afraid of him. If I didn't comply, I was afraid. He would do various things to hurt me. Once he broke up my sleigh with an axe before my very eyes.

KENT: How long did that last?

VERONICA: Well, when I was twelve or thirteen, he finally accomplished penetration. Then I was into deep sexuality. I had guilt feelings because I was attracted towards the act, the sex act itself. But emotionally I was torn because the wrongness of it entered my mind.

KENT: Were your aunt and uncle involved in any church?

VERONICA: My aunt used to take me to church when I was small. They wanted to rest on Sunday, so I was put out and sent to every Sunday school in the area just to keep me away from the house. I had a lot of Sunday school teaching when I was small. Perhaps that is where the concept that the relationship was wrong came from. I don't really know, Kent.

KENT: Was your aunt aware of what was going on?

VERONICA: Obviously not.

KENT: Veronica, you are talking about having real conflict. You were having intercourse with your uncle. What developed after that?

VERONICA: I was quite an intelligent person. When I was young, I had a great thirst for knowledge. Unfortunately, the country I was from, with its class system, made it difficult to go on to higher education. If you had parents who had little money and couldn't get a scholarship, you couldn't go to a higher education school. When the examination came along I wasn't brilliant enough to win a scholarship and they weren't willing to put the money out for me. At grade eleven I had to quit school and I started working. This is when I was nearly sixteen. All this time the relationship was going on between my uncle and me. I think I watched the "Life of Christ" on TV once, and I was really drawn to God; I really felt love for this man, Jesus. So I went around the house hunting for a Bible and I found a New Testament. And like everyone else who is searching, I started at Revelation. It is the hardest book in the Bible, but it brought a sense of awe in my heart. And I started praying. I felt guilty about the relationship with my uncle, but I felt trapped. It was like I was in a cage. I was very young and afraid. I wanted out, but I didn't know what to do. I had very little contact with my father, brother, and sister. My uncle was afraid, I guess, that I would talk. So there

41

was very little contact with the family. I hardly ever saw them. So I had no one to turn to except the Lord. I used to sit by my window at night and pray that God would help me because I couldn't handle the situation. It got so bad that I considered taking my own life. In fact I did try. We had some phenobarbital in the house and I took six half-grains. I thought it was enough, but it wasn't. I was very drowsy for two days. It was enough to frighten my uncle so that when I said no, he backed off. I said no, and I really meant it. For a whole year we lived in the same house and never spoke a word. As a person he was just there, and I was there. And for that whole year there was nothing between us. I think he realized I was getting older and it was too dangerous to push the issue.

KENT: Veronica, I know that was hard for you. You left home then when you were seventeen?

VERONICA: I ran away, more or less. I wanted to be a nurse very badly. But most of all, I wanted to get out. I felt that I was being crushed by the whole thing.

KENT: During all this time with your uncle, had you ever had any boyfriends?

VERONICA: No, because he wouldn't let me. I had no friends of my own age at all—no girlfriends, no boyfriends.

KENT: You didn't consider yourself homosexual?

VERONICA: I didn't even know what it was. I was very ignorant about sexuality. I thought it was a man-woman thing. I never realized that men or women could have sex with each other. I mean, we came from a small village and I was never exposed to that sort of thing.

KENT: How did the homosexuality develop?

VERONICA: Well, I was in training at the time. . . .

KENT: Training to become a nurse?

VERONICA: Yes. The training school was fairly far away from this particular girl's home and I had nowhere to go on weekends anyway. So we both stayed in the training school on weekends. And it was the first weekend. She was not a homosexual but when you are seventeen you talk about boyfriends and sex. I was very curious because I never had a boyfriend. And I was talking to this girl and I said, "Well, what do you do on a date?" She said, "We kiss." And I said, "What else do you do?" "Well, you know," she said. "He runs his fingers down my back." And she did it. She showed me, she held me close and that was when I realized how tender a woman was. And no one had ever held me tenderly. I became very attached to this girl. I was just like—I don't know how to explain it. There was nothing sexual about it. It was a sort of worship-type crush. This was the first time I realized—

KENT: You realized there could be some kind of love from a woman. But you didn't identify this as homosexuality.

VERONICA: No. I still didn't realize that homosexual relations were possible. Nothing else happened with this girl. I finished training and I went back to the main hospital. Then I met another girl. This is a different girl who was not a homosexual either. We were in bed together talking and stuff—

KENT: You mean girl-girl stuff?

VERONICA: Yes, a girl-girl thing, just talking and stuff and I kissed her. And I felt, um, this is different. By this time I was going out with guys, but I didn't like them kissing me or touching me. I just wanted to get to

43

know them as people. But that is kind of difficult. I kissed her and everything my uncle had taught me before seemed to come back automatically. You know what I mean—the fondling, the stimulation. And that is how it started. But I wasn't really in love with her. It was a friendship. But it grew and grew. We got an apartment together sometime later, and this sexual thing came up.

KENT: It became more and more a part of the relationship?

VERONICA: Yes. But I had this feeling inside that it wasn't good, wasn't right, and that it was offensive to God. I didn't know where this conflict came from. It was something that I felt inside.

KENT: Did you recognize this as any kind of homosexuality?

VERONICA: I still couldn't put a label on it. I just knew it wasn't right. In fact she had a cross on her neck and I tore it off of her and threw it into the fire. I told her she shouldn't be wearing it. I identified the cross with goodness and purity, which I didn't have and neither did she. I put a stop to the relationship. She had fallen in love with me and I couldn't cope with the attention. I didn't want that kind of relationship, really. So I put a stop to it. But we stayed friends.

KENT: At this point, you hadn't identified yourself as a homosexual. When did the idea begin to develop that you were different?

VERONICA: This relationship lasted for about three years, but the sexual part was stopped after the first year or so. I was going out with a guy, and we were talking about getting engaged. I couldn't figure out why I didn't have a deep love for him. But I thought it would eventually develop.

KENT: Had you gotten involved with him sexually?

VERONICA: No. He respected me and wanted to marry me. He was really a good-looking guy. I never felt I was pretty or attractive. And when he really liked me it did something for my ego. And so this was going on, but I realized that I just didn't love him. I wanted to go away for a while and do something different, think it out. So I moved to Sydney and I started my midwifery there. The first day I was there, there were twenty-five of us in a room and this girl, whose name was Sara, walked in. And when I looked at her I fell in love with her right away. I liked the way she looked, the way she carried herself. She was very, very pretty. She was sophisticated and beautiful—everything I wanted to be. That is when I realized that I felt differently about this girl.

KENT: Did you feel this was homosexual?

VERONICA: I felt this for the first time. I was friendly with a girl who had gone to boarding school and she told me some of the things that went on. She said girls fall in love with each other and never get over it. For this reason she would never send her child to boarding school. Her words sunk into me and I realized that was how I felt about Sara. That is when I realized I was different because I couldn't eat, couldn't sleep, and I cursed God for making me this way.

KENT: You felt mad at God because you were different?

VERONICA: Yes, I was mad at God. I said, "It is your fault, you made me this way."

Three of us shared two beds and we used to rotate. One got to sleep alone while the other two had to share

45

a bed. One day I woke up and Sara put her arms around me and started fooling around. To me this was really serious. Even though I wanted to, something held me back. I got out of bed and turned away. And the relationship never developed into anything; it was really nonsexual.

KENT: This was occurring when you were how old?

VERONICA: Just twenty-one.

KENT: Did you enter into any other relationships?

VERONICA: No. I was doing my training as a midwife and we had to go out to our districts. This meant a move. I still had not found my sexual identity, but I was still going out with boys. I was quite popular you know, and I never had any trouble getting dates. We used to go to parties and stuff. Religion and God hadn't entered the picture. I always had the image that God was someone out there you thought about at Christmas, but that He had no concern for me as a person. But then I went on district and met two girls who were Christians. I could immediately see there was something different about them.

KENT: And it was through these two girls that you became a Christian?

VERONICA: They didn't actually witness to me. Nothing like that. I could see by their lives that there was something different there. So I went to church and I said, "Lord if you are really real, then you can have me." That was all the transaction that I did.

KENT: What happened after your conversion? Did you get involved later in the homosexual life?

VERONICA: Well, not for at least two years. It still hadn't clicked that I had homosexual tendencies, until I met another girl when I was twenty-four and fell in love with her. And I expressed my sexuality with her, and that is the first real experience I ever had.

KENT: Were you beginning at this point to identify yourself as a homosexual?

VERONICA: Yes. I didn't want to be that way, and I knew God didn't want me to be that way, but that was the way I was.

KENT: What did you do with your Christianity at this point? Did you still continue to go to church?

VERONICA: I tried, but after I got into this thing with Leah, that was her name, I realized that I couldn't go to church and have her. So I had a conflict.

KENT: You left the church?

VERONICA: Yes.

KENT: What was the result of this?

VERONICA: Well, as I said, I never had a lot of guilt about having sex with a woman, though I felt it was wrong. Even though I was not going to church, I was still trying to be a Christian. I would pray and read the Bible. The Spirit was still alive in me. And Leah had put a stop to our relationship because she had been a Christian. That hurt me a lot, but I got over it. Again, I started to go to church. I never felt at home in a church, I always felt I was kind of worldly and they were so pious. They had no make-up and wore ugly clothes, and I liked nice clothes and cosmetics. I identified Christianity with long skirts, no make-up, and piled-up hairdos. I decided I couldn't really be a Christian because I wanted to have a relationship with a man, and there were no Christian men available in the church. But in the world there were men, so it wasn't just the homosexuality that pulled me away from the church. It was the desire to go to parties, and

47

go on dates.

KENT: It was hard for you to identify with the Christian life style?

VERONICA: Yes.

KENT: It seems like you were in and out of churches.

VERONICA: Yes, that is true. But now I became involved in various gay relationships. Really into it all.

KENT: Could you tell me, Veronica, how long ago it was that you made a real break from the homosexual life?

VERONICA: Three years ago. Nearly four now.

KENT: Can you tell me briefly, what brought that about?

VERONICA: I started to lose my sexual identity when I was twenty-six, and began to pick up male mannerisms. You know, crossing your legs, and lounging around. My feminine identity was being crowded out with the gay relationships I was having. Then four years ago I had a real bad time with a lover. My world was closing in on me. I realized at that time my only hope for living was in Jesus because my desire for living was gone. I made such a hash of my life that I didn't know any real happiness. I was confused, and yet I knew that God was the answer. When Joan left me I went back to the Lord. I remembered reading in the New Testament that people had thrown out their magic books and burned them. And I thought I'd try that. So I stayed in my room and said to the Lord, "I'm renouncing all of this life style, this homosexuality, and I want you to help me be the person you want me to be. I know it is going to be awfully hard, but I believe that you can do it. I believe you, Lord, because I trust you. You have been with me the last eight years when I have failed you so much." He was always there when I came back to Him to pick me up and comfort me. Jesus Christ was the answer and I knew that if I gave Him a chance in my life, there was a possibility of real change.

KENT: Was it at this point that you began to identify with the church?

VERONICA: No, I still felt that I had failed God so much that my witness for Him was gone. Therefore I thought I couldn't belong to a church. I had this skeleton in my closet. And it wasn't until about a year ago that I began to deal with this skeleton. Every time I wanted to do something for God, Satan would come along and say, "Hey, remember you are a lesbian." I was afraid that somewhere along the line I would meet someone who would say, "I know you, you used to be gay." I wanted to deal with that so it wouldn't be hanging over my head.

KENT: What did you do, Veronica?

VERONICA: What did I do? I started praying to God.

KENT: You are saying that for about three years you were a Christian all by yourself.

VERONICA: Yes, I was.

KENT: You weren't going to a church. But what about friends in the gay life. What did you do about them?

VERONICA: You see, the Lord in His mercy made them not want to see me. I tried to contact them and form relationships because I still cared about them as people. But they wouldn't have anything to do with me. They didn't want to see me, write to me, talk to me.

KENT: That is quite a miracle.

VERONICA: That is!

KENT: You didn't have a difficult time pulling away from the gay life style then?

VERONICA: No, not at all.

KENT: What kind of problems did you begin to experience then?

VERONICA: The problem was a sense of personal worth. You see, I had lost that. I had lost the sense that I was a valued member of society. And I was terribly lonely.

KENT: You were living by yourself?

VERONICA: Yes, I was living by myself. I had a house and I spent all of my time on my own.

KENT: Had you moved to Toronto by this time?

VERONICA: Yes, this is when I moved to Toronto. Joan left me, but I stayed put because I had a real good job and a good reputation as a nurse. At the hospital they valued me and I wanted to stay.

KENT: How about your sex drive?

VERONICA: I masturbated sometimes. But the Lord convicted me about that. Then I would argue with myself, "How can it be wrong since I am not involving anyone else?" But I couldn't quite be honest with myself. I realized it was a selfish act. Other people weren't telling me, this was just the Holy Spirit. I wish I had known somebody I could have told my past to. Someone who would have understood and accepted me as a person, and helped me deal with my problem. I went through it all alone and that was very difficult. It really was.

KENT: Especially the loneliness?

VERONICA: Especially the loneliness and the lack of goals for my Christian life. I wanted to serve God, yet I didn't know how to do it. I thought I had wrecked my life for Him.

KENT: What was it that brought you to a place that

you started to be involved with other Christians?

VERONICA: The Lord first brought my conscious attention to homosexuality and the reasons for homosexuality through the gay liberation movement, and especially an interview on television with various gay liberation women. I felt a compassion for them; I knew what it was like to be in love with another woman. I felt bad that nowhere in the church could I see any ministry to people who had problems such as I did. I started to read material on gay people. I didn't know of anyone ministering to gay people, but I didn't believe I could be of any use in this ministry. I had to find something to do with my life. I had given up on sexuality; I wanted something that would meet my needs as a person. So I started to look to the university and a master's degree in nursing. And that is when I found your book, *The Third Sex?* I had holidays coming up at that time and I went away for a week. I read the book and felt I needed to talk to you. I read the introduction of your book again and found something I had missed before. I found out about the fellowship. And I thought if I could talk to somebody about my past I could get rid of this dark cloud that was hanging over me. You know the rest. I phoned you that day, bought an airplane ticket and came to San Rafael. We had a series of interviews and I got rid of all the depression and feelings of guilt.

KENT: There were lingering guilt feelings. You needed confirmation by other people who knew Christ and who knew your background that you were a child of God whom He wanted in His service.

VERONICA: Yes.

KENT: You are coming to be with us?

VERONICA: Yes, pretty soon. Praise the Lord, I am.

That gives me greater satisfaction and peace than I have ever known.

KENT: I am excited that you are going to be with us and serve in our ministry, Love in Action. Let me ask you one of the most common questions. How do you deal with temptations?

VERONICA: They don't go away completely. I knew I was dealing with more than my own old nature; I was up against a spiritual power, too. I knew I would be challenged and tested. When it came, I was ready for it. It was very difficult for me, and it was very difficult to say no to someone who loves you. I didn't allow relationships to develop. There was one friendship that could have destroyed me just after my return to Christ. I helped bring the person I was involved with to Jesus. I felt responsibility toward her. I didn't want to hurt her. This meant turning away from any sexual involvement. In the beginning it did happen, but it wasn't deep. It was more of a hugging closeness which gradually develops, but I put a stop to that anyway. Having faced temptation and overcome it, its power is much weaker now than it was before.

KENT: The repeated refusals to give in have a cumulative effect.

VERONICA: Yes, there is a growing strength. Yet it doesn't go away. I have to consent in my will daily to stand against homosexuality. I know I must turn away from the stimulus, and deal with it by bringing it out in the open and saying, "Okay, this is what's happening, and it just can't be!" Determining in my will to turn to God makes a major difference.

KENT: Obedience?

VERONICA: Obedience—that is the word!

KENT: Do you read the Bible and pray now?

VERONICA: Oh yes, all of the time. I always did read the Bible. But now I read it and pray daily. I find that is my greatest strength.

KENT: Right now do you feel you have any problems relating to homosexuality?

VERONICA: I don't like being rejected. I like to be accepted as a person. And there is a lingering fear that, as soon as I make my background known to other Christians, they will reject me. But I have learned to deal with that in the way that I love gay people. I have been there and I know what it is all about. I desire to reach out and help them. I am helped in dealing with the fear of rejection by saying, "Lord, I am doing it for you. I am not going to accept this feeling of rejection because it is Satan's way of discouraging me."

KENT: Veronica, do you think you will ever be married?

VERONICA: Yes, I do. Anyway, I hope that I will, now that I am beginning to rediscover my sexual identity as a woman.

KENT: You told me once that you are becoming more feminine.

VERONICA: Yes, I have learned that I don't mind male attention any more. That feeling of threat from males is gone. I realize through Jesus Christ that they are human beings just as mixed up as I am about things. And I realize that the declining morals in the 1960s had a lot to do with my fear of men because they expected me to be a sex object.

KENT: You enjoy being a woman more now?

VERONICA: I enjoy being a woman. I feel comfortable with men who are heterosexual. I don't mind their attention. It is not a threat to me because I feel comfortable with my sexual identity. Now I am beginning to dress as attractively as I can because I like it. I like being a woman! And hopefully I believe the Lord will restore me as a whole person.

KENT: How about your sense of self-worth? Have you had to struggle with your value as a person?

VERONICA: I did up until I met you six months ago. Now I realize I am not unique. There are millions of others who have this problem. You helped restore my feeling of self-worth. I stopped looking at myself. You said something that stuck in my mind, that the Holy Spirit had protected me from a lot. I realize that now and I am praising God that He kept me from so much. And the fact that I can be of use to Him in reaching gay people is the greatest feeling of self-worth. My worth to God has been restored; therefore my worth to myself is restored. That is the whole relationship, that is most important to me anyway.

KENT: You are looking forward to ministering to lesbians. Do you think you can relate to men who are struggling with the gay life?

VERONICA: Yes, I relate to them very well. Through our group here I am relating a lot to them. As a matter of fact, I am learning by being involved with men who have had gay backgrounds. I relate to them as people and I see they are struggling with their own identities. They have hurts, pains, and they feel sorrow. I see that our spirits are exactly the same; we just happen to be in different kinds of bodies.

KENT: Yes.

VERONICA: I am relating to men more on a spiritual and emotional level where I couldn't before because that thing of the body was a threat to me.

KENT: Veronica, is there anything at the end here that you would like to say?

VERONICA: It is always wise to remember that what God has said is the most important thing. And God has said, "Male and female He created them." If we have the roles mixed up, it isn't God's fault—it is the fault of man—our fault. I do not mean man, male; I mean man as a whole, society in general. It depends on the training we have, the decisions we make, and what we are exposed to that confirms our sexuality. If we have it all mixed up, God in His love can do a miracle in our lives.

KENT: Thank you, Veronica, for sharing this interview.

4
Interview with David

KENT: David, would you please tell me about your background, your age, and so on.

DAVID: I am thirty-seven years old. I was born in Seattle and spent the first three years of my life there.

KENT: What were your parents doing?

DAVID: My dad was a storekeeper.

KENT: Your dad was a storekeeper at that time and you lived in Seattle until you were three.

DAVID: Right. The funny thing that I might mention was at that time I had a fear, sort of, of people.

KENT: At three?

DAVID: Yes. Also there was an attachment to males at that time.

KENT: You were conscious of that at three?

DAVID: Yes. I am not inferring that there is such a thing as a born homosexual, but I believe at that time things had developed in my family so that my orientation was being formed in a homosexual way.

KENT: Did you get along well with you father?

DAVID: No. As I was growing up there was always an alienation between my father and me. There were times when he and I would be close to an extent. He would take time with me, talk with me, joke around with me, and take me for a ride somewhere. Most of the time it was a struggle with my father. I never really felt that he liked me nor that I was wanted in the home.

KENT: Are there other members of the family?

DAVID: There is a brother.

KENT: Older or younger?

DAVID: Older. And there is a sister also. She is older. They could do no wrong.

KENT: You were the squirt?

DAVID: I was the squirt. I came along ten years later.

KENT: Did you ever think your birth was an accident?

DAVID: I thought about it. Much of the time that my mother was alive (she died when I started into my teens) she would repeatedly confirm to me that I was a wanted child. Because of that, I didn't believe her.

KENT: You grew up in Seattle. As I remember you moved around from place to place. And now you are living where?

DAVID: San Jose.

KENT: And briefly, what kind of work do you do?

DAVID: Accounting.

KENT: Would you tell me about your school years, the grammar school period?

DAVID: All through school I went through a number of experiences. I was a person who enjoyed life, that is, outside of my own family. And I enjoyed going places and I enjoyed the life around me. The trees, the birds, the flowers, the dogs and cats. I was very suspicious of people and their motives and certainly the responses of the world today have confirmed my suspicions. But I didn't have a lot to do with children much before I went into the first grade. And in the first grade I had a girl friend.

KENT: You had a girl friend. Do you remember her name?

DAVID: Yes. Her name was Barbara. Barbara and I, how should I say, related to one another most of that school year. Then in the second grade I was blessed with no less than three girl friends simultaneously. That, of course, didn't last very long. And in the third grade on I was without.

KENT: Why is that?

DAVID: I don't really know. I can't quite answer that because it is a little vague to me. But circumstances perhaps at home and in school were such as to start me to withdraw. And I did not and have not associated with people much except that I get to know them and realize they are on the level.

KENT: Evidently, David, you withdrew a lot when you were young.

DAVID: Well, as I say, it was my feeling that there was little I could do to please my father. And my brother and sister were always teasing me. I had an inferiority complex at the time and felt that I wasn't worth anything and that I wasn't wanted. My brother and sister played this hard on me, whether they realized it or not. In fact, one of their big tricks was to get me in some sort of circumstance and then let mother and dad know about it. Now they claim they could do no right, but it didn't look that way to me. I always felt like I came out on the short side of things.

KENT: The result was you began to withdraw.

DAVID: Right. The only person I trusted was my mother. And throughout the school years I did develop friendships. Interestingly, in none of those friendships was there any tendency towards a sexual interest. My close friends were not the people I would have gotten involved with in a sexual way. But there was developing through the junior high school years a strong orientation toward the same sex.

KENT: Can you pinpoint any reasons why this began to happen during your junior high years?

DAVID: I think it probably goes back to the fact that I so much desired to have a true father-son relationship with my dad and a brotherly relationship with my brother, not only as blood relatives but as friends. Now I praise God today that my brother and I are friends, and that my father and I are friends. But my father knows the Lord now, and he did not back then. He was also under much stress due to a rather poor financial situation in the home. I was not aware of that. Through my teens they kept things from me. The more they kept things from me, the more I distrusted them. It was general knowledge that my mother had cancer, but they never told me until just a few hours before she died. They could have told me before, but they never did. And when they did, it wasn't a very pleasant experience.

KENT: The main reason you see for liking other guys is that you hadn't a relationship with your father or your brother?

DAVID: Right. I craved to have some kind of a relationship. Also, at the onset of puberty I had a lot of sexual fantasies. When I started to develop sexually, I was looking for an emotional and sexual outlet. Of course, the sexual outlet could have been kept where it belonged if there had been a proper emotional outlet with a man. But it was not to be found in the home. In fact, when neighbor boys came over they were more welcome than I was.

KENT: David, did you get involved in sexual activity with any of your young girl friends?

DAVID: No, I did not. The only sexual activity I had with another person was when I was about thirteen, with a close friend of mine. And that was the kind of thing most boys go through. An experimentation kind of thing. Only I could see it going beyond experimentation with me. I wanted to pursue it.

KENT: David, was this with a girl?

DAVID: No, it was with a boy.

KENT: This was when you were thirteen, the first time you were ever involved with someone sexually.

DAVID: It was never brought to fulfillment.

KENT: Just an experimentation?

DAVID: Yes, but I desired more of that kind of thing. It was a strong thing with me. Masturbation was a very strong factor for me for many years in my life. This was accompanied always with much fantasy.

KENT: Homosexual fantasy?

DAVID: Yes. I will say in my high school years there was a girl who showed up in one of my classes one day. And that girl impressed me. For three years I could not keep my eyes off of her.

KENT: She must have been something.

DAVID: She was. We got to know each other. Perhaps a relationship could have come out of that. But because of my emotional problems, not homosexuality, it didn't work out. I think the homosexuality would have gone up in a cloud of smoke had the personality problems been taken care of. We might have entered into a relationship. And there were times when she was the subject of my fantasies. I always felt guilty about that because I have always held women and marriage very sacred. Even at those times I had very idealistic, very high standards about marriage. I was disgusted with marriages because I did not see people working to solve their marital problems. Yet I kept thinking that deep down in my heart it was possible.

KENT: You held women highly; there wasn't a hatred toward women. David, let me ask if you thought of yourself as being homosexual?

DAVID: Yes, I did, but I never really acknowledged it. I never came right out and said I was. I was aware there was a problem.

KENT: Did you know about homosexuality?

DAVID: Oh, yes, very definitely.

KENT: You learned it in school or around the community?

DAVID: Yes, as a matter of fact one young man who happened to be the son of a prominent minister in town was the wildest person I think I ever ran into. He was a pathetic case. During junior high school he was frequently in trouble with the police for homosexual activities in movie theaters and places. Often he would call my house. He would follow me home from school. I lived five or six miles from school, and I had to walk clear across town. He would follow me long distances and hide behind buildings when I would turn around. I was not afraid of him.

KENT: Because of this boy you came to have an understanding of homosexuality?

DAVID: Yes, he broadcast it to anyone who was in earshot of him. However, before this boy, I imagined all of the sex activities of homosexuality. Those things were fantasized in my mind before I ever experienced them, or heard of them. I wondered if anybody else ever had such bizarre fantasies. To me they were very bizarre. Maybe they came from the powers of darkness.

KENT: It very well could be, David. Interesting point. Now, at this time did you begin to identify yourself as homosexual?

DAVID: Okay. When I went into the military service, of course, I was exposed to nothing but men and under very close living. Unknown to me, there were overt homosexual acts all around me. I did not see them and I would have been too fearful to have gotten involved in them. Now I thank God for that fear. It kept me out of a lot of trouble in those days. I do also want to mention that I left the military service for a short period of time and got involved during that period with a nice Christian girl. She was head over heels for me. I got scared because I could see her pushing for the altar and I wasn't to be pushed. I thought she was a nice girl. She was a cute girl with a good personality. I thought that it wouldn't be bad, but I was scared.

KENT: Did you ever have any sexual relations with her?

DAVID: No, and I don't know if I would have done it outside of marriage at that time. So what happened then is I reenlisted in the navy. While stationed in another country, I went to a resort hotel for a weekend.

KENT: Prior to this you had never been involved in any homosexuality?

DAVID: Not any actual act. Although I really abhor drinking I did it because I was a lonely person. I wanted so much to relate to individuals and I could not relate unless I did what they did. And so drinking got involved. There were many servicemen at the resort hotel and I met one young man in particular. And there was just something there. I couldn't quite understand it but I thought at the time, to myself, that he was homosexual. We got acquainted, drank together and he asked me to go to his hotel room. So I did and that is where it happened.

KENT: That was your first experience?

DAVID: Right.

KENT: How old were you at the time?

DAVID: I was twenty-three.

KENT: I want to back up a bit, and ask you about any religious influence in your life.

DAVID: Very good. That is a very strong point. I thank God that my mother taught me to pray nightly. If nothing else she taught me to pray the Lord's Prayer. I did for years. Then I had a prayer that I prayed to God for everyone in my family and myself. I prayed always for God's protection. And I cannot even tell you the number of times God had spared me when I was a child. God puts His hand over children and protects them. He is longsuffering and full of mercy.

KENT: You had a relationship with the Lord even as young child.

DAVID: I did not know Him as my Lord and Savior. I never heard anything of salvation until I was thirty-one

63

years old. But my parents went to a Presbyterian church. I got into the Presbyterian church especially in my late high school years. I went to church on and off because I reverenced and feared God, but I did not know Him. I knew that Jesus Christ was God, but that was where it was.

KENT: I hate to jump back and forth in your life history, but what was the effect of that first homosexual experience? What did you think at that point?

DAVID: I was saying to myself right in the middle of the whole scene that this is what I had always dreamed of. It was a fulfillment of what I had fantasized in my mind. And there is a school of thought that says if you fantasize something long enough, you will do it.

KENT: And it will become reality?

DAVID: Right. After that I began a downward spiral in my life and things happened to me that were devastating. I thought God was punishing me and I was reaping the judgments I had asked for. That experience left me feeling guilty, but I desired more.

KENT: Did you think you should not engage in homosexuality?

DAVID: No. I went three years after that without any involvement. I then developed a friendship with a young man that I had met in the service. It was a very intense friendship. If we had known the Lord, we would have had the kind of relationship that Jonathan and David had, a real genuine love, brother for brother. This man was almost like a brother to me. He was a very sexually oriented person to me. He would swing both ways. We came very, very close to sexual involvement.

KENT: But you never were sexually involved with him?

DAVID: No. He thought it would do something to our relationship. We did have an extraordinary friendship. Later on, he married. He was away from his wife one weekend in another town and called me and wanted me to come see him. I think this was after I was fully involved in the gay life. I think he wanted me to get involved with him that night, but I wouldn't do it.

KENT: At this point you began to involve yourself seriously in the gay community?

DAVID: What happened was that I got out of the military in San Francisco. Well, here is where it all happens. Shortly after I went to Southern California for a while. And down there I read books, heard stories, saw ads in newspapers. That was all I needed to know. From there on I was hitting bars in Hollywood, all over Los Angeles, and finally all over Los Angeles County. I got involved with many, many people, including people in high places. Oh, yes, I want to say something I was going to let pass. While in the military I did get involved sexually with prostitutes, bar women, in the Orient.

KENT: Did you like those contacts?

DAVID: Some. Some were just a sexual release. Masturbation was far superior. I mean, with those women it is nothing more than getting up in the morning or having to sweep the floor. There was nothing satisfying there. I think that is why most military men go for each other because at least they can find some kind of emotional involvement. Anyway, I got involved quite a bit in the gay community.

KENT: For how many years?

DAVID: I better back up on something. There are two other things I want to bring up about what happened after I got out of the navy. I got involved with a prostitute in Southern California. She chased me all over town and I wanted nothing to do with her. I know I could have gotten on with women. But I feared going to bed with women because of venereal disease and pregnancy. Even if you didn't get them pregnant, all I ever heard of California girls was that even if they weren't pregnant, they would accuse you of it. And there was another girl, a neighbor of mine. I got pretty close with her until she told me she was married. She was a sweet girl. Then I saw this whole thing with women was a tremendous trial. The kind of woman I would like to have, where could I find her? You certainly don't find them in a bar. Finally I got to the point where I was convinced that my life style was to be homosexual.

KENT: You accepted your homosexuality and were willing to stay there.

DAVID: Right. I got actively involved in a homosexual life style. And when I say actively, I mean it. I was into every facet of it that I could get into. For six years.

KENT: Now David, what is it that began to bring you out of the gay life? What are the events that led to your conversion?

DAVID: Okay. What happened was that at the same time I got involved in the gay life, I met many people in high places. Many people in Hollywood. Some of my friends got me involved in the occult.

KENT: What forms of the occult?

DAVID: Eastern religion, but also spiritualism.

KENT: You mean spirits and seances?

DAVID: Right. When I came to the Bay Area I got involved in a spiritualist church. It was supposed to be a Christian church, if you can imagine that. I got to telling a fellow worker about this and he in turn would tell Christian believers about it. I knew this man had accepted Jesus Christ as his Lord and Savior, but I did not know anything about the Holy Spirit. He would listen to me as I told him all the occult, spiritual hogwash, thinking I was way up there in spiritual knowledge. He would listen and listen. He was so loving to me. And then as soon as I would leave he would call people on the phone and ask them to pray for me. People I did not know would pray for me. I believe that had a lot to do with it. Before I was even born again the Lord delivered me from the occult. I renounced it. I began going back to my Presbyterian church then. I used to go to church, then cut out of there and go to the nude beaches. On one occasion, I don't know why, I happened to stop at another kind of church, and for the first time I heard the gospel of Jesus Christ. It is funny that I had never heard that in thirty-one years. And when I heard that message I made an altar call after the service.

KENT: There was an invitation at the end of the sermon and you responded to that?

DAVID: I made that altar call and received Jesus into my heart. There was no follow-up after that, no one talked to me about it, and I didn't know what it was all about. When I walked out of there I didn't know what to do with it. The result was, of course, I backslid right away. Even worse. I got into the darker and grosser aspects of homosexuality. I backslid and really got into those deep dark things. I was very involved sexually again. One night I felt that what I was doing was not in agreement with God, and I told Him so. It was just like God was saying to me, "Now is the time to renounce all this." I got down before the Lord and received Jesus into my heart. I really did. I gave my life to Him and gave up those particular aspects of sin. I decided from now on anything I had to do with homosexuality was going to be within the bounds of a proper lover relationship. I was bubbling over with joy. I was saved and I knew it.

KENT: But you didn't yet know that homosexuality was wrong?

DAVID: No. That is strange but I must admit that even before I was involved in the gay life style I read in the Bible that Paul said, "Men doing that with men which was unseemly." And I remember being right in the middle of a sex act and thinking to myself, "If this isn't unseemly, then what is?" But that didn't stop me. But there were times when my eyes were open. Anyway, I asked God what I would do about a church. You see in 1969 I had gotten involved in the Metropolitan Community Church in Los Angeles.

KENT: Your involvement in the M.C.C. was prior to your conversion?

DAVID: Yes, prior to my coming to the Bay Area. At first I thought that it was a nice thing. Later I began getting discouraged with it. So when I came to the Bay Area I had a roommate who pleaded that I get involved in the M.C.C. in San Francisco. But when I got saved, I asked God to take me to the church He wanted me to go to. You know the strangest thing happened. It was at the M.C.C. in San Francisco that I met people who led me to meetings not related to the

68

M.C.C. where I received the baptism in the Holy Spirit. At the M.C.C. I was involved sexually with other gay people there. I still wasn't convinced that it was wrong. I felt that there could be a proper kind of relationship in that scene. But as it was, some of these people were used of God to take me to meetings where there was teaching on the Holy Spirit. The Holy Spirit is a comforter, but He is also a teacher and an enlightener. And I believe that when He comes into our lives He really shines the lights on.

KENT: It was after this experience that you began to see into the nature of your homosexual life?

DAVID: One day a brother in the Lord told me that homosexuality was an abomination to God. This brother was not gay. Something came up about homosexuality and he did not know I was gay. He told me the Bible, the Word of God declared it. When he said that, the Holy Spirit gripped me inside. I could not wait to get home. I got down on my knees and prayed hard and asked God for the truth. I got the Bible out and saw exactly what it said. It was plain; there was no question about it. It was in black and white. Then I prayed, "Lord, I want everything you have for me. I want to be right before you. I want nothing, absolutely nothing in my life that is displeasing to you. I believe you paid for everything on the cross. I believe your blood was shed for my diseases, all of my hang-ups. I give this to you and I ask for deliverance from homosexuality in the name of Jesus Christ."

KENT: After that very powerful event were you tempted with homosexual fantasy or desire again?

DAVID: I wanted Jesus and I wanted to do right before God. I knew what His Word said about homosexuality. So I cut it off. I totally cut off from it. Everything and everybody, people and places, I did my best to put it behind me. I figured I had to turn around and walk completely away from it. That does not mean that I did not have problems with my sexual drive. My sexual drive would swell up and there would be fantasies and masturbation. Every time it happened I repented and asked Him to strengthen me and lift me back up.

KENT: How did you relate to straight Christians?

DAVID: That is where a problem came in. I don't know if the problem wasn't compounded by the fact that I had known rejection from people generally and lacked self-confidence. I knew God had delivered me even though I might have thoughts or memories. I was free from it. I believed with all my heart that I was heterosexual. I was a new man. Other people might see something in me that would give it away. Or they might find out about my past. They might find out about something from somebody else if I got established in a church. Eventually a young man came into that church whom I had known previously and he told everybody that he had a problem with homosexuality. I was sure he told everybody about me. Because of that, it was difficult for me to relate to people. I knew that, although many people loved the Lord, there is a terrible stigma about homosexuality. They might look down on me. Even though I knew I was free, they might not.

KENT: But you knew that going to church and being a part of Christian fellowship was essential.

DAVID: Yes. That did not drive me away from church. I still went and got involved. If people knew, maybe some of them did, they never let on. They were what the Bible said Christians should be. They were open. There were some who probably knew and I felt they regarded me with a jaundiced eye. The pastor knew because I told him when I came there that I had been delivered from homosexuality. I was more than welcome in that church.

KENT: Do most of the people in the church know of your past, David?

DAVID: The majority of the people know in the church because I am involved in this type of ministry. But some people may not. There are many people in our church, interestingly enough, that I was afraid might find out about me and reject me, who turned out to have been involved in homosexuality themselves. Many of them had married and I would have never guessed they had been involved in it.

KENT: Now you are married. How did you meet your wife?

DAVID: After I walked out of the gay life and started coming to church, I found that the sex drive doesn't stay behind. I wanted to fulfill this in a proper manner. I was also a lonely person and I believed in a home and marriage. I wanted to get married. One time I happened to be in the home of a brother and sister in the Lord who had greatly befriended me. I didn't feel it was edifying to tell them about my past. This brother and sister took me into their home and really loved me. He knew that I had this inclination to want to get married. He said to me, "Brother, I think you need to realize that you don't really want to get married. That yearning in your heart has been placed there by the Lord and it is for marriage, all right, but it is for a

71

marriage relationship with Him. He is wanting to show you that you need to develop that very relationship with Him, to be in love with Him. Once you do that you will see the desire fade away until the proper time." That hit me. I came home and got down before the Lord again. I began to develop a relationship with Jesus that night. As I established that relationship with Him, the desire did go away. Things in my personality, my character, scars, memories, bitternesses, and disappointments began to be worked on. If I had gotten married at that time it would have been a disaster. I was not ready for it. My personality was not ready for it. It would have been a tragedy. It is by no means easy to come out of homosexuality and the only way is through the blood of Jesus Christ and wanting that relationship with Him. There is no other way. You cannot dive into a heterosexual relationship; that won't do it. It is not a quick cure-all.

KENT: You were converted in what year?

DAVID: In 1972. It was early 1973 that I started on this marriage kick and my friend set me right. And through that time God dealt with me in many ways. As I began to grow in the Lord, there came a time when the thing came back on me about a year later.

KENT: What came back on you?

DAVID: The desire for marriage. "Oh, Lord are we going through this again?" I thought. "Are we, or am I now quite in the right relationship with you or what?" This time I saw that it was a right desire. I would go to church and pick this one or that one. I would say to myself, "I will take this one, and if she's not available I'll take that one, and if that one is not available I'll take this one." I had them in a certain order, down to the least desirable. All I was looking at was the fenders and the hubcaps, the hardware and not the person. I was only thinking of myself and all that. It finally got to be a frustration. I got disgusted with it and went home from church one time after an evening service and said, "Lord, I am fed up with all of this. I want to be married and I believe it is your will for me to be married. But if the marriage is not put together by you, it is not worth anything. You know me better than anyone does and you have a woman that is right for me. You know her. Lord, you do the work in both of us and bring us together in your timing. You pick her out. Your way is perfect." It was something like that. I was going to try to keep out of the way. I figured that if nothing happened by the time I was thirty-six then I would forget about it and resign myself to remaining single. I was just about to turn thirty-four at that time. Well, then in the summer of that year, 1974, I happened to meet my wife.

KENT: And her name is June.

DAVID: Right.

KENT: David, was she going to the church?

DAVID: Right. In fact during a morning service the whole congregation was worshiping the Lord and the Holy Spirit just kind of said, "Open your eyes." I did, saw this woman, and felt, "Oh, no." I closed my eyes quick. He said, "Open your eyes again." I thought, "Oh no, she is down on the list somewhere." I opened them again and I saw her. I saw a beautiful, sweet precious little woman who loved Jesus Christ. So when I opened my eyes a second time I said, "Yes, Lord, I see what you mean." I dated her three times. I took her out to dinner one night and I was sold.

KENT: Did you ever reveal your background to her?

DAVID: I was very concerned about that. I went to my pastors and they told me it was under the blood so leave it there.

KENT: So they advised you not to tell her.

DAVID: And we prayed that God would cover it, and that was that. Unknown to me, her mother knew about me. In God's timing, we got married.

KENT: Did you have any trouble relating sexually?

DAVID: No, no; it was beautiful, just beautiful. That is why when I said I let go and let Him handle the situation instead of me trying to fight it, it was fine. I was always concerned that she would find out. Sexually there was no problem. But then in early 1974, because of people coming into our church who were gay, the pastor called upon me to be of some assistance. And when I started to get involved in this type of ministry, the question came up that my wife was going to find out about it. What was I going to do? And the pastor said that I should get that matter out of the way. So I went home and told her. At that time we had been married for fifteen months. I said, "I have to tell you something. I have been ministering in the church to homosexuals because the pastor needs some help in this area. I want you to know something. I have been there. And the Lord set me free." She looked at me for a second and said, "You have? I have been there too!" And she had not known anything about me. She was surprised.

KENT: You were surprised as well?

DAVID: She thought she was the one coming out of the background to marry some nice, straight Christian fellow. We are both straight and normal heterosexual

74

people because God did it. That showed the miracle of the Lord and the completeness in His work of delivering people. Not only from homosexuality but from many other problems. From my experience, the real key is wanting to be free. And if a person wants to be free, the Lord will do it.

KENT: David, for some years now you have been actively involved with gay people who come into the church and then seek help.

DAVID: Right.

KENT: This has been important to you. Knowing what I know about you, I see that the church and the ministry has been a very important part in your stability as a person.

DAVID: Yes, I would not have been able to do so well had I not gotten established in a good, Christ-centered, Bible-believing church. I believe that once a person comes to Christ and then asks for help out of homosexuality they need to get into a good church where they can receive solid teaching. It strengthened me.

KENT: I see on your desk a picture of a little boy. How old is he?

DAVID: He is now eight months old.

KENT: I saw him when I came in. So you now have a nice family, and you have your church, and a regular job as an accountant. God had done a lot of work in your life. I know that you are reaching other people. I want to thank you for the time you have spent with me and for personally involving me in your life.

DAVID: God bless you.

5
Problems
of the Former
Homosexual

The response that the book, *The Third Sex?*, has received since its publication has been intense. An evaluation of the many letters and phone calls has shown that more needs to be said about the tests, trials, and troubles a former homosexual faces and how such problems can be dealt with. This is the intent of this entire volume, but is especially true of this chapter.

Not being a homosexual, I am not competent to speak to the inner struggles a person faces as he follows the way of the cross. Our Love in Action group, former homosexuals who regularly meet together, has, however, given me a great deal of help. They have expressed to me the major difficulties they have faced, the conflicts, the failures, the anguish and the excuses, so that I could address these problems with confidence and authority.

Upon their conversion, several of the members of

our fellowship group experienced a miraculous deliverance from the desire for sex. They were on a spiritual high. It was as though God had placed them in His hands to shelter and cradle them. This resulted in a dramatic change, a euphoric state that carried them through what might have been very difficult times. They were safe and free, even to the point of boasting they would never be affected by homosexuality again.

Then God set them back into reality. His sheltering hands, it seemed, were removed and it was real life again. The experience was still true, Jesus was their Savior, the church, and the Christian friends too, but the victory seemed in jeopardy. That spiritual high they thought would last forever was gone. At this point, some were in a state of panic, others were mad and disappointed. Cries of "Unfair," "Why me?" and "Let me out," would thunder up from within. Life was once again hard to cope with. And the sex drive reappeared. The craving for sexual gratification became an increasingly dominant need.

Some reasoned they were abnormal, thinking that everyone else was doing well but that they were especially weak. Desperate thoughts crept in, thoughts of having committed the unpardonable sin or that they were not worthy to be Christians. The experiencing of the sex drive again produced extreme ideas, such as, "God has abandoned me," "I may as well give up," "This life isn't for me," and "Now I can never be forgiven."

A common experience at this point is to be entrapped by lust. A girl in our fellowship called me one day. "Kent, the best-looking butch just walked by and could I go for her. What do I do?"

Others, faced with the harsh truths of reality after coming out of a period of spiritual security, have looked at the Christian life with disdain. Jesus, who had seemed so wonderful, now seemed a threat. The Christian life, which had been so beautiful, was viewed as a great burden that deprived and restricted them. They felt singled out for a crushing blow that others, especially heterosexuals, did not experience and could not understand.

Actually many new believers, homosexual or not, experience a wonderful spiritual high upon conversion, and are brought back to reality by a loving God who knows what is best. When this happens, several principles can be applied which can be of great help.

One, dig into the Bible. There is no substitute for diligent Bible reading and study. The Word of God is the reality the Spirit wants for us. Our hearts must be open to receive truth that is uncomfortable and calls for change in our thinking and behavior. It is especially important not to compromise on God's revelation about homosexuality. Let God's truth remain truth for you always.

Two, honestly face your situation. Effective prayer demands honesty. If the good warm spiritual feelings are gone, admit it to yourself and to God. Being able to say, "What happened to the Holy Spirit?" or, "Why is this happening to me?" is essential in order to be able to pray, "God help me, things are bad." If you have a minister or Christian friend that you trust, be honest with this person also. Being able to tell another person about it can be very helpful. You can tell God, or a man or woman of God, that you're mad, depressed, sexually starved, lustful, confused, tempted beyond reason, or whatever, and not be rejected.

Three, know the truth about temptation. First of all, God never tempts anyone. Our own sinful desires are the real source of the temptation (James 1:13-15). We must know where the temptation is coming from in order to properly deal with it. It is nothing to be tempted, it happens to everyone. Secondly, we can escape temptation. God always provides a way out, if we are looking for it. (1 Cor. 10:13). He will help us endure it though there may be suffering. Thirdly, there is forgiveness if we yield to the temptation. God's attitude is: "I don't want you to sin because I love you. I desire that you be perfect and holy as I am. But if you sin, I have made a way out for you through my Son Jesus, that if you confess to me your sin, earnestly desiring to turn from it, I will completely forgive you." Remember that God's love reaches even into the pit of death.

An interesting occurrence that is observable in laboratory test conditions, but also applies in psychological fields, is called "extinction." Dave Engle, who graduated from Oklahoma State University with a degree in zoology relates how a northern pike was placed in a tank of water at the water condition closest to its normal environment. Minnows were fed to the pike daily for him to eat at his pleasure. Then one day they enclosed the pike in clear plexiglass; he charged at the minnows trying to eat them, and banged his snout on the plexiglass, until finally the pike quit trying to eat any minnows. After the plexiglass barrier was removed, and the minnows were able to swim freely around the pike, the pike starved to death. His aggressive attack had become "extinct."

For a habit pattern to become extinct, God in His infinite wisdom will place the plexiglass barrier around us, but we must bump our noses against it. As we face each encounter, praying to God for help, for strength, for courage, we'll find that each temptation gets smaller and smaller until it finally vanishes.

Four, don't be surprised when you experience suffering. Jesus suffered, and when we walk in His steps, we will suffer too. Suffering is not unusual. Everyone who attempts to lead a Christian life will suffer. Having to be celibate after months or years of homosexuality is difficult and involves suffering. But suffering that is endured actually builds up and produces strong character, a solid personality. It is not unfair that we should suffer, either. It is one thing to suffer for the name of Jesus, but another to suffer as the result of a sinful past. Everyone experiences suffering too, not just the homosexual.

Five, learn to praise God. It is easy to be thankful on the spiritual mountain top, but God desires we praise Him in the valleys as well. In His Word we read, "Give thanks in all circumstances, for this is the will of God in Christ Jesus for you" (1 Thess. 5:18). This is contrary to our fallen nature. Usually we are not thankful anyway, but God wants us to praise Him regardless of how we feel. This can pick you up out of self-pity. The former homosexual can feel singled out, so put-upon by God and the church that he can wallow in an enormous cesspool of self-pity. Praise demands a shift of center from self to God. One cannot praise God without relinquishing his or her preoccupation with self. God asks us to turn our hearts and minds on Him with a word of praise on our lips. Notice too that it is God's will that we praise Him. Praise, even when we detest the idea, brings the Holy Spirit's presence right into our problem to work in ways far beyond our capacity.

Five, be filled with the Spirit (Eph. 5:18). This, again, is God's will. When a homosexual turns from homosexuality, a great void is left. He may have an extreme, abiding sense of emptiness and loneliness. Only Jesus and the fellowship of His people can satisfy that desperate inner hunger. So many have verified that the Holy Spirit can so fill a person that their greatest needs have been satisfied.

Great men and woman of God, like St. Francis and St. Theresa, have found that God gives wonderful love and joy to those who live the celibate life. Our Love in Action fellowship group demonstrates the same. God's love for us is immense, His Spirit all-powerful, His grace all-sufficient. He wants us to be in love with Him, to yield to the fullness of His Holy Spirit. This is the Lord's plan for the normal Christian life.

These are helps in leading a normal Christian life, not a formula for perfection. Yet these points are real, biblical, and workable. The Christian life is sometimes very hard, but God, by His Spirit, is able to work miracles in our lives when we let Him.

In talking to the fellowship group about special difficulties that homosexuals face, celibacy and its problems were often mentioned. As I listened, it seemed to me that they felt only former homosexuals had to deal with giving up sex. The truth is that many people live without sex. There are those who have remained single and celibate for the sake of the gospel. Being celibate out of necessity for ministry is an honorable decision as Paul points out in 1 Corinthians 7. There are others who are celibate due to physical injuries or disease. There are widows and widowers, divorced people and single people. In my own church there are well over a hundred young adults who have made decisions to remain sexually right before God and wait for marriage. God honors the celibate life, we ought to also. Unquestionably these people face temptation and sexual frustration. My pastoral counseling experience shows me this is true. It is not just the former homosexual who is asked to turn away from sex. And to look at it from a slightly different perspective, it is better to be celibate and deal with sexual temptation than to indulge in sexual sin and lose the kingdom of God.

It is difficult not to live for today only. The homosexual life is often an intense drive for satisfaction and happiness. Christ's love and life is intense, but it is not physical and sensual. It may seem a poor substitute for the immediate gratification experienced in sexual indulgence. The former homosexual must make a transition in his life here, moving from a life of continual questing for sex to a life of faith and obedience. There is no question that this is hard. The feeling is that the Christian life simply is not as good. It is essential that the former homosexual submit himself to Christ and His discipline, and consider himself dead to sin. As Christ becomes more real, the strong pull to the frantic searching for the right sex partner decreases. As love for Jesus grows, the need for the counterfeit love falls away. The former homosexual must sincerely seek God's kingdom first and foremost.

Counseling designed for the alcoholic taught me a great principle of living moment-by-moment with Jesus. When the alcoholic was asked if he could live twenty-four hours without a drink, he replied, "No." "Well, can you live twelve hours without a drink?" Again he replied "No!" "All right, can you live two hours without a drink?" "No," he said, "I don't think so." "Okay, can you live five minutes without a drink?" "That's silly," he said. "Anybody can do it for five minutes." For ten years he has been without a drink, and it started five minutes at a time.

To compensate for rejection and to establish a secure identity, homosexuals often develop highly sophisticated lifestyles and attitudes. Once a person is converted, this sophistication can actually stand as a barrier that separates him from other Christians. This is especially true at first. Those just coming out of a life style exclusively homosexual who have adopted a superior attitude and a sophisticated orientation often have difficulty adjusting to Christian fellowship. Often they miss much of what they need to grow in Christ because of this barrier. The former homosexual must withstand the temptation to reject Christian brothers and sisters who are "straight." There can be a significant distrust of anyone not gay. It is in this situation that we most clearly hear God's word in Scripture,

> Welcome one another, therefore, as Christ
> has welcomed you, for the glory of God.
> (Rom. 15:7)

The sharing of any type of essential character with others is self-perpetuating, especially if we say to ourselves, "This is what I am." We would be freer if we said, "This is what I do." What I do leaves an option of a future, of hope, through change. An ultimate freedom is to renounce an "identity" and realize that we are what we choose and wish to become. We must choose a new life style, our old identity is to be replaced by a new, Christian, God-centered identity.

Fetishes can be a particularly rough problem for former homosexuals. Fetishes may be highly developed. It may take years to come to a place where the sight of a foot, an ankle, shoulder, or whatever the fetish might be, does not provoke a sexual arousal. A deep spiritual commitment is required to overcome highly developed fetishes. It is recommended that a person so troubled confess the fetish to God, ask for an emotional and mental healing, and earnestly strive to stand against every pull to the fetish. Again, the victory in this area may not come at once.

I have talked with several people who have turned to Christ thinking such a commitment would transform them from homosexuals to heterosexuals. This doesn't automatically happen. One young man who became a Christian desperately hoped he'd be genuinely attracted to a girl who loved him. He lapsed into intense bitterness toward God when the miracle didn't occur. The thought that such a miracle is impossible, of course, is not true. In trying to force such a change, some have entered into heterosexual affairs. To replace one sin with another can be devastating. Sin is sin; sexual sin is sexual sin whether it's homosexuality, adultery, or fornication. The affair with the opposite sex is fraught with all manner of dangers such as rejection, self-hate, and guilt. This is no way to overcome a problem. God, in His time, in His way, will work into our lives that which is needed.

It has been my experience that a change from homosexuality to heterosexuality is worked out as a process over a period of time, perhaps a long period of time. I cannot say that a homosexual will assuredly ever come to a place where his identity is strictly heterosexual. It is true that positive growth does occur, but the possibility of never moving to heterosexuality clearly exists. To think that a person must become heterosexual is not warranted. The pure motive for turning to Christ must be to glorify God, to turn from sin, and enter into a faith-relationship with the Father. Biblically speaking, the faith that pleases God and works salvation is not simply the desire to be heterosexual. We must come to God without condition, and especially without the intention of bargaining. We come to Him as sinners, lost and in need of forgiveness and salvation. If a person is saved and has problems that last a lifetime, it is worth it to gain Christ and spend eternity with Him. The Psalmist said,

> I would rather be a doorkeeper in the house
> of my God than dwell in the tents of
> wickedness. (Ps. 84:10)

In a counseling session recently, a young lesbian told me, "I'd rather be living with a girl than be alone and masturbating." She was weighing the alternatives, and the thought of being alone and without a sexual outlet was disturbing. Being young she was wondering if she shouldn't stay in the gay life for a few years; then, when she was older and had experienced all there was as a homosexual, she would turn from it altogether and be a Christian.

This is a genuine problem for younger homosexuals. In one meeting of our Love in Action fellowship, three young men attended who had never had sex but considered themselves homosexual. One by one, the core members of the group earnestly sought to help these young people avoid a spiritual blindness that would result in their crossing over the barrier that protected them from the gay life. We had learned that Satan commonly tries to deceive by using the old hack, "Try it for a while and then you can get out of it." Sin does blind; continual sin brings great darkness. Guilt diminishes eventually until a deep pit has been dug. This is a serious matter. There can be no compromise with sin. We must accept the truth that sin produces death and have the security and courage to follow Jesus even if loneliness and sexual frustration are a result. Paul wrote:

> For his sake I have suffered the loss of all things, and count them as refuse, in order that I may gain Christ. (Phil. 3:8)

Satan, the adversary, must be reckoned with. It has not been uncommon to hear a former homosexual say that he had never had so much sex available as when he turned to Christ. Sex that had seemed unattainable before became easy, almost thrust upon him. Why? One reason could be the devil. Scripture tells us that Satan earnestly seeks someone to devour. Our spiritual warfare must not be dismissed. The enemy is real and the believer is the target. God tells us to flee youthful lust and to resist the devil. This is affirmative, positive action on the part of the Christian.

Anyone involved in a gay life style usually has a weak will when it comes to sex. Barriers normally strong against assault have long since crumbled. When Satan throws easy sex at the new Christian, hard decisions are called for. The ensuing battle can be terrific, but with each "no" to sin and "yes" to God, Satan is progressively robbed of his victory. He wants to take advantage of the weak will and get the former homosexual back. And, Satan or no Satan, as human beings we have the capacity to assert our wills over our emotions. Obedience is centered in our wills, the faculty in which our decision-making takes place. God wants our will submitted to His so that our will is His will.

Sexual fantasies must be rejected. Though they descend without warning, they must immediately be stopped. To indulge in sexual fantasy is to open the door to real sexual sin. You can't walk in the Spirit and engage in lustful fantasy at the same time. Fantasies grieve the Spirit of God and separate us from His abiding love. What we think about all too often becomes reality. Jesus taught that out of the heart comes evil thoughts and sexual sin. Giving oneself to lust and sexual fantasies is to invite real trouble. As fantasies are confessed and rejected, as our minds become captive to Christ, fantasies have less and less influence.

Every believer, former homosexuals included, must reckon himself dead to sin. He must strive, with all the strength the Holy Spirit gives, against sin. The battle is intense, but Jesus does give victory. Our formula for triumph over Satan is "Submit yourselves therefore to

God. Resist the devil and he will flee from you (James 4:7).

The homosexual cannot change without the power of the Holy Spirit. God's Spirit works in our lives as we yield to Him, recognizing that on our own we have little power to turn from sin. Before Christ we were dependent on ourselves. Now, with Christ, we depend on Him. Two key signs of dependence on Him are prayer and moment-by-moment walking in His presence. Jesus, who indwells every believer, goes with us always and is constantly there to meet our needs.

Resentment against God is often experienced by the former homosexual. This may arise from believing that God is unfair to have made them that way or to have given them such a heavy burden. They may feel bitter that they are not normal like other people.

We know that it is unreasonable for us to blame God for our own sin. Emotionally, however, our experience may be to the contrary. It is common for persons suffering from grief reactions that follow the death of a loved one to feel angry at God. The loss of a homosexual identity, estrangement from gay friends, and the loss of a lover may also produce a grief reaction. Something has been gained but something has been lost. It is helpful to know that God continues to love us even when we are mad at Him, and that after a period of time, resentment and anger towards God will fade.

The gay life style can produce a pattern of lying; one is forced to live by a lie. There are the stories of girlfriends, boyfriends, dates, engagements, divorces, all designed to deceive and pacify the heterosexual world. However, when Christ comes into the homosexual's life, He calls for honesty. Having lived dishonestly for so long, it is difficult to make the transition. Lying can become an enduring method of dealing with people, even in the church. It will cause barriers to go up and alienate the former gay from fellowship with other Christians. Lying must be dealt with severely. One sin, like lying, can lead to other sin. Alcohol and drug use may have been prominent in a person's life, since much of the gay life is centered in clubs and bars. Alcohol and drug abuse must be rejected as well. One person who would occasionally come to our Love in Action group maintained that he didn't feel it was necessary to stop going to the gay bars. He didn't want to stop seeing his old friends and was attracted to the atmosphere of the bar.

As Christians we must be clear as to what is involved. We are not to continue the same old life style of sin that was so attractive. God's word is that we are to "come out from them" (2 Cor. 6:17), even if old friends reject us. We are to be separated people. The old attitudes and sin must be strenuously rejected in favor of fellowship with Christ and His church. To compromise here is dangerous. Jesus warned against putting new wine into old wineskins. If you try to do so, the new wine will be lost as the old skin bursts. God has provided a new life and a new environment, a life with Jesus in His body, the church. From Psalm 1:1-2 we read:

> Blessed is the man who walks not in the counsel of the wicked, nor stands in the way of sinners, nor sits in the seat of scoffers; but his delight is in the law of the LORD, and on his law he meditates day and night.

The old friends of one of the members of our group kept after him to return to the gay life. They accused him of searching for homosexual contacts within the group. He was severely put down for his Christian stand. Though they were old friends, they began to withdraw from him. The attitude was, "What a weird thing you are into. When will you grow out of this new trip?" Bitterness and resentment was expressed since the Christian witness was a threat to them; they had to attack or give in. Their goal was to get him back in the old comfortable life of sin. Gradually this new believer was without friends and was worried whether the Christians would receive him. It was a struggle of faith.

What happened to this person in our fellowship group happens to many others who turn from homosexuality. They are almost in a "third world," neither heterosexual nor homosexual. Unless there is a Christian fellowship to be involved in and Christian friends to spend time with, the former homosexual can experience extreme loneliness. It is at this point that one must actively seek out believers to fellowship with. Risks must be taken to give Christians who know nothing of homosexuality a chance. Though the church is not perfect, God does not intend for the former homosexual to exist in a vacuum. The Lord has provided the church for fellowship, protection, and an environment for growth in Christ. It is important then for one to move out of a "third world" situation and identify with the family of God.

There are special problems a former homosexual faces as he begins fellowship with Christians. One is that some Christians and even leaders will be closed to relating to anyone associated with homosexuality.

There is a fear involved that is difficult to explain but that every former homosexual is sensitive to. I have found well-meaning Christians incapable, at first, of accepting someone with a homosexual background. In church meetings, testimonies from converted murderers, prostitutes, narcotics dealers, and Satan worshipers are often heard, but the testimony of a former homosexual is rarely heard or sought. This is unfortunate. The church needs to hear this witness that Christ delivers from homosexuality too. Facing the problem of rejection in the church requires courage, and God does give strength to do this. Walls may be up at first, but God's Spirit of love can break them down. It might be necessary to conceal one's gay past at first until the climate is right. The benefits of Christian fellowship are worth the risk. Even facing the fear of possible rejection from others in the church helps to break down well-established patterns of withdrawal and hiding. No one is meant to stand alone. The wolf always picks out the straggler. Get in fellowship because God wants you there, and He'll make the rough places smooth.

God's promises are everlasting and are ours to claim. Isaiah 58 tells us that God honors our service and self-sacrifice to others. Becoming familiar with these passages by studying and memorizing them will help you to utilize them in your daily life. 1 John 1:7 promises fellowship as we walk in the "light" and our light shines in our service to humanity. Idle time, idle minds, are Satan's workshop. In addition to losing ourselves by laying aside our own selfish desires, we need to continue to study God's Word, memorize it, and incorporate it into our educational studies, street work, politics, ecology, or other occupations we may be involved in. Allow God to bring into your life the fellowship He desires for you.

Another problem was expressed by a girl in our fellowship group. She confessed she felt guilty being with other Christians. If there was anyone she wanted to get close with she feared that her expressions of affection and caring would be misinterpreted. She wondered how close you could get and still have everything remain all right.

The Bible teaches us to "love one another with brotherly affection," and to "greet one another with a holy kiss" (Rom. 12:10; 16:16). There is a place for innocent, genuine expressions of love and caring in the church. Affection does not have to be sensual. It is a revelation to many that this is possible. The former homosexual needs this warmth and affection; it is a sustaining factor. They should enter into it boldly under the guidance of the Holy Spirit. Satan may use this to bring temptations, false accusations, and guilt trips. But one should not listen to the "accuser of the brethren," rather, reject the enemy and claim the right to brotherly love.

A third problem concerns the new relationships established in the fellowship of Christ. Many people who have been thoroughly involved in the gay life are strangers to family life. It is common to be jealous of families. The impact of the cost of living a homosexual life may be severe as family love and solidarity is observed in the church. Even the dedication or baptism of infants is a hard thing for the former homosexual to endure if he feels as though he will never have a family. And then there are a myriad of confusing feelings that are experienced as friends in the church pair off and are married. The former homosexual can feel utterly left out and alone.

These feelings must be faced; they can not be avoided. Perhaps the former homosexual will never have a "normal" family or be married at all. Fortunately, we have the confidence that God gives us exactly what we need. He knows our fear and the longings that go unfulfilled. He would satisfy them with himself. The love of Jesus surpasses any love, the fullness of the Holy Spirit satisfies more completely than any earthly, physical relationship. The future in Christ is also full of promise and hope. God through His prophet Joel said, "I will restore to you the years which the swarming locust has eaten" (Joel 2:25). We must learn to praise God for all He has given us and resist looking back or concentrating on what is lacking. Praise to God is His will for us in all circumstances.

6
Ministering to the Homosexual

The church in the latter part of this twentieth century is faced with a great opportunity and challenge. I don't think anyone can deny that there are many people in our society who refer to themselves, or feel that they are, homosexual. If we are going to minister in this kind of a world, if we are going to be servants of Christ today, we are going to be ministering to the homosexual. It is almost unavoidable. A pastor told me that he would refuse to minister to homosexuals, and I happen to know that in his congregation there were several homosexuals already. He was in fact ministering to them, through his sermons, his Bible teachings, and so on. The man of God will minister to those God brings to him. I am convinced that the church has the means, the only means, of dealing with the problem of homosexuality, the sin of homosexuality. And for that reason I have a burden on my heart to share with people a little bit of what I've learned about ministering to those who are caught up in homosexuality.

I am not an expert, neither do I think anyone is ever going to be an expert on homosexuality. I don't want to seem as though I have all the answers. It's a very difficult kind of ministry. I've been involved in ministry to alcoholics. I spent three years in the Haight-Ashbury district working with runaways and drug addicts. But ministry to homosexuals is the most difficult form of ministry that I have ever known. And I know that I don't have all the answers to this particular problem. But I do know it is one that the power of the Holy Spirit through Jesus Christ can deal with and I believe that while the Holy Spirit moves in the church, and as the gospel of Christ is proclaimed, the church has the means to bring life and hope to a person who is faced with this sin. So I am actually addressing this to the church. This chapter is not aimed at the homosexual per se. It is directed to my colleagues, my associates, my brothers in Christ, who are involved in trying to minister to people who are dealing with homosexuality.

The first point I'd like to make is that the church *can* minister to the homosexual. It is quite common to hear men in Christian leadership express their feelings of inadequacy in this area. A common retort is that the homosexual is so crippled psychologically, emotionally, spiritually, that he cannot be reached.

In 1973, through a counseling ministry we have in our church, I became involved in counseling with homosexuals. I hadn't encountered this situation before. Not being a homosexual, I had no inkling as to how to deal with this, nor had I read anything about it. I was as unprepared as anyone could possibly be. Counseling for me was simple pastoral counseling. I knew how to tell a person about Jesus and apply biblical principles to a person's life to help in dealing with everyday situations. Certainly I am no clinician. In dealing with the homosexual I was just out of my realm. But I was confronted on a personal counseling basis with several people telling me they had problems related to homosexuality.

Over the years then I have discovered that it is possible to minister to this problem. The church is able to do it. Men whom God has called to be His ministers in the church can deal with it and even extend life, new life, to such people.

There are four primary ministries the church can extend to the homosexual. The first of these is *forgiveness*. There are two passages of Scripture that are extremely relevant at this point. First of all is 1 John 1:9, a very familiar passage of Scripture. It says, "If we confess our sins, he is faithful and just to forgive us our sins, and to cleanse us from all unrighteousness." I think it is very well accepted that this first letter of John's is written to the church. And John says, "If we confess our sins." He is writing to Christians who are sinners, just as I am a sinner, and just as every other Christian is a sinner. He is writing to these people telling them there is hope if we confess our sins.

And this verse may be coupled with 2 Corinthians 5:17 where Paul says, "If any one is in Christ, he is a new creation; the old has passed away, behold, the new has come." We see the very clear biblical principle that God is a forgiving God. God forgives because he loves us, because He wants to bring us back into a relationship with himself. So standing before all of us, standing before the person faced with the problem of homosexuality, is forgiveness. Due to the fact that God in Christ has taken our sins on himself at the cross, He is ready to forgive our sin, wash all of it away. Since the blood of Jesus Christ has been shed, every man stands in the place of forgiveness dependent upon confession and repentance of sin.

Another extremely important passage along the line of forgiveness is 1 Corinthians 6:9-11. It reads:

> Do you know that the unrighteous will not inherit the kingdom of God? Do not be deceived; neither the immoral, nor idolaters, nor adulterers, nor homosexuals, nor thieves, nor the greedy, nor drunkards, nor revilers, nor robbers will inherit the kingdom of God.

Before we look at the eleventh verse, I would like to make these comments. That list of sins speaks to all of us. I can speak for myself on a number of these. And I am sure that any honest man is going to see himself in this passage as well. Now the homosexual is grouped right in there with everyone else. Paul says, "Do not be deceived." Who can say they have never been deceived? How about being immoral? Jesus talked about lusting in the heart, and says that it is the same as adultery. Who has not done that? Who has not at one point been greedy? None of these shall inherit God's kingdom. Look at the eleventh verse. "And such were some of you. But you were washed, you were sanctified, you were justified in the name of the Lord Jesus Christ and in the Spirit of our God." This is a tremendous passage for all of us. I get excited when I read this Scripture because it tells me forgiveness is a real possibility for every man. Any person who has ever lived stands in the place where God's love can reach in forgiveness. Notice it says you were washed. There were homosexuals in Corinth. They were washed, sanctified and justified. To be washed is to be made clean. Many people feel homosexuality is such a "dirty" sin. Washed is washed, and it is by the blood of Christ. The washing is so thorough it makes us white as snow. In Isaiah 1:18 it says, "Though your sins are like scarlet, they shall be as white as snow; though they are red like crimson, they shall become like wool." To be sanctified is to be declared holy, set apart for God. The regenerate homosexual is just that. In addition, he is justified; that is, he is made righteous, free from the penalty of sin. All this belongs to any sinner who repents to God and commits himself to Christ. The church must claim this for the born-again homosexual.

The church can minister to the homosexual because of the forgiveness that is available through Jesus Christ. It is not possible to move from homosexuality into the Christian life without forgiveness.

One of the incredible things that the homosexual experiences is guilt. We know that guilt is one of the big problems people face today. It is a primary cause of emotional illness, depression, and so many of the ills that plague people. And the homosexual is particularly plagued by guilt. In Christ we see freedom from guilt through forgiveness.

Freedom from guilt and other consequences of sin is dependent on the experience of repentance. Persons coming out of homosexuality are often unaware of the wide consequences of their sin. Initially they may simply be weighed down by the burden they carry. Men of God need to help them repent thoroughly. There are many factors to consider. For example, homosexuals usually live a fraudulent life style, especially before family, co-workers, and neighbors. They are forced, in a sense, into living a lie, telling lies to cope with their circumstances. Ray Hession in *Forgotten Factors* (Fort Washington, Pennsylvania: Christian Literature Crusade, 1976) calls this "multiplied duplicities." All of this deception must be repented of, as well as the wrong done to others. Homosexuals, especially those who have been active in the bar scene, have indirectly affected the lives of many, many people. This factor must be recognized. Christ's freedom comes with genuine, thorough repentance.

The second thing the church has to minister to the homosexual is *acceptance*. We know that the fellowship of Christ is a fellowship of acceptance. Those people who have done a lot of counseling realize the tremendous effect that rejection has on a person, especially the young. It is during the formative years when a person experiences rejection. It is commonly experienced in a divorce situation. A young person who experiences that kind of rejection in their childhood will often rebel. Homosexuality is a result of rebellion. It is in fact the most extreme form rebellion can take because it is acting in exact opposition to the way God created us. It is very important to the person who has been involved in homosexuality to receive acceptance. They have rebelled against any sort of authority that has been around them and they will anticipate rejection from the ministers of the gospel. Perhaps whatever the form their rebellion has taken leads to more rejection. They have been rejected by the straight society and have experienced rejection in the homosexual society, and what they need to experience is acceptance. In the *koinonia*, the fellowship of the people of the church, we have the great melting pot. We talk about America being the melting pot. Well, the church is the melting pot of all the sinners. And in the church there is the acceptance the homosexual needs.

When a person turns away from the old homosexual life to follow Jesus he is going to lose all his friends. If such a person does not receive acceptance and welcome into the fellowship of Christ, he will end up being isolated and lonely. We know that part of evangelism is an invitation to fellowship. John talked about that in 1 John 1:3. He said, "That which we have seen and heard we proclaim also to you, so that you may have fellowship with us; and our fellowship is with the Father and with His Son Jesus Christ." It is the place of acceptance, the place where a person can be received and welcomed, not on the basis of what he has done, but because Jesus Christ has made him new.

Paul in Romans 15:7 says this, "Welcome one another, therefore, as Christ has welcomed you, for the glory of God." Those of us who have the wonderful opportunity to minister the gospel of Christ welcome one another even as Jesus has welcomed us.

The third thing that the church can minister to the homosexual is *love*. Again that's the welcoming theme, the accepting, the receiving, the confirming of the fact that God has forgiven this person and made him new.

Outside of Jesus Christ I could never love a homosexual. That may be a shocking statement, but I remember how I was prior to my conversion. I was the kind of person who would like to have harassed them. I used to hear about some of the guys at school hassling the homosexuals down in Los Angeles and would think that was just terrific. Christ began replacing whatever it was in my heart that came out as anger against homosexuals with a genuine love for them. Love is one of the wonderful things that the church can minister to the homosexual. Not a love on our own, it is a love on a godly level, agape love. It's impossible without Christ. There is just something about the love of Christ. We receive that love ourselves and it helps us to love others.

And then the fourth thing that the church can minister to the homosexual is *power*, the power of the Holy Spirit. The word deliverance is talked about a lot today. In terms of the homosexual this is a key concept. Sexuality is the very center, the very core of our humanness and for the homosexual this is very true. But the homosexual is a slave to his sexual impulses. To be delivered from that kind of slavery, the power of the Holy Spirit is required. And those people in our fellowship who have come out of a homosexual life style give a very strong witness to the power of the Holy Spirit. Very often I have heard people say that if it had not been for the miracle of God's grace and power they could never have hoped to move away from their homosexuality.

With these four tools—forgiveness, acceptance, love and Holy Spirit power—the church can minister to those people who have given themselves over to the sin of homosexuality.

The second point I would like to talk about has to do with the existence of the Metropolitan Community Church, better known as the "gay church." Founded in Los Angeles by Troy Perry, its ministry is aimed at the homosexual. However, it does not preach repentance from the sin of homosexuality. Their theological stance is one that negates the very clear Scripture that speaks of homosexuality as a sin. It then basically offers people religion and homosexuality too.

The M.C.C. has experienced incredible growth. It is growing and will continue to grow. The very fact that the M.C.C. exists and has grown tremendously shows us that thousands, actually tens of thousands of people in the homosexual community, are looking for the truth, are looking for the Bible, are looking to ministers, are looking to the church for help. It has been my experience to find people caught up in the M.C.C. who really had a heart's desire to have a personal relationship with God. I have encountered members of the M.C.C. who had been Christians in their childhood, had subsequently become homosexual, and had gone to the M.C.C. because they didn't feel there was anywhere else to go. But there was this hunger, this desire to know God, that all men, if they were honest, would admit to having. So the fact of the existence of the M.C.C. leads me to believe that those of us in the church today actually have a field white unto harvest amongst those who are involved in homosexuality. Because of the book *The Third Sex?* and the letters that we have subsequently received, we have found that all over this country, as well as in Canada and Britain, there are hundreds of people who are telling us that they want to know Christ, that they want to be in a church that will receive them, that they want help in moving away from homosexuality. Tragically, we know of few places where we can confidently direct them. We urge them to seek fellowship, and they and we realize it is quite risky. And so I think that there is, as the second point, a field of ministry that is wide open for the church of Jesus Christ today. I think it provides a tremendous opportunity to reach people who are looking for the truth.

The third point I would like to make is that homosexuals are people. Prior to the beginning of our Love in Action ministry, I shared the view many people have that the homosexual is some kind of strange creature who is to be avoided at all costs. Now, let me share with you that homosexuals are just people. I would say to any pastor reading this that if you have a congregation of a hundred fifty or two hundred people, I would imagine you have some people who are either homosexual or are former homosexuals right in your congregation. And they may be people that you know, respect and like. My point is that homosexuals are people, but they have a sense of isolation because of their fear of rejection. They are reluctant to admit their problems. They may struggle on for years and years wanting help but afraid to seek it. Though they feel isolated, they may have a desire for their ministers to know they are just people and that they didn't have to be afraid of them. Homosexuals are people, made in the image of God, made with a capacity to know and to love God. They are people for whom the Lord Jesus Christ shed His blood on the cross. They are people who can be as special, precious, worthwhile, and lovable as any

103

person who has ever lived.

My fourth point is that there is great fear in regard to homosexuality. I have tried to isolate two different kinds of fear. The first is the fear that the homosexual experiences. Secondly, there is the fear that those in the church experience. The fear the homosexual has, as previously mentioned, is the fear of rejection. In the homosexual community, according to the pro-gay publicity, there is much love and acceptance. In reality there is a lot of rejection. The homosexual is rejected in the gay community, and he is rejected in the straight or heterosexual community. In different counseling sessions I recall people trying to muster up the courage to tell me that they had a homosexual problem. I knew it by various hints they had dropped, and I saw them struggling, fearful of letting me know they were actually homosexual. For those ministering to the homosexual we must know that they have a tremendous fear of rejection.

The homosexual may be afraid of losing his job. This is a very real fear. Sometimes the work is the only stable factor in his life and he is very aware of potential scandal or blackmail. People whose homosexuality is discovered are often in danger of losing their jobs. So there is the fear that the straight society will reject him and cause a great deal of upset.

Another area of fear for the homosexual is rejection from friends in the church. For example, there was a young man troubled with homosexuality who was a member of a particular church and had a tremendous desire to communicate his problem to his pastor. But he held it back for years because he was afraid of word getting out into the church. He feared he would lose friends he had worked so hard to gain. As we minister to people, then, who have homosexual problems we need to exercise a high degree of confidentiality so a person has the security in knowing that his past sins will not be broadcast about in the church, in addition to showing genuine acceptance.

Then there is the fear experienced by the members of the church, including the leaders. Heterosexuals are repulsed by homosexuality. I think that this is beyond dispute. It is not an unnatural thing but it should not prevent ministry being extended toward the homosexual.

My wife and I from time to time would talk about homosexuality. We asked ourselves, what do homosexuals do? I didn't even know. I had no understanding of what homosexuality was. It was something I didn't deal with. I was afraid of it. And when I began to minister in the area of counseling to the homosexual, this fear came to the forefront of my mind, too. It was something I had to overcome, and it wasn't easy. It took months.

There were all kinds of fears that I had. For example, I thought if I started ministering to homosexuals they would start coming to our church, and maybe they would molest somebody, perhaps get to some of the Sunday school kids. I didn't know how to deal with this sort of thing. All sorts of possibilities ran through my mind and it really produced a fear. I thought that if we started ministering to homosexuals then our church would be called the gay church. People might even drop out. I could hear it being said,

"Don't you know that all kinds of homosexuals go there?" Our church was in the process of growing, God was blessing it, and I thought perhaps this was Satan's device to destroy us. All these fears came to my mind. I know, too, that some ministers fear to face ministering to homosexuals since it causes them to confront their own sexual insecurity, or homosexual tendencies. This would be quite common and not a great barrier to overcome. These kinds of fear God must help us through if we are going to be able to minister to the homosexual.

The remainder of this chapter is addressed to the question, "How might a door be opened to minister?" Basically there are five things I would like to say in regard to this. I want to look at three ways in which this ministry might be opened up, discuss a caution, and finally, give an explanation of the ministry we call Love in Action.

First of all, I would suggest beginning with the process of education through teaching and preaching. I believe I would approach it in this way. I would first preach a sermon or two on sin, in which I would include homosexuality. And I would speak of homosexuality as a sin; I would speak of it as something that has to be turned away from, repented of, but also that it was a sin like any other sin.

The Bible contains a complete picture of sexuality as God ordained it. Homosexuality needs to be presented as it relates to God's creating man male and female. In the Book of Genesis, we see heterosexuality to be the norm with homosexuality being an expression of missing the mark. It is essential to make very clear that the sin of homosexuality cannot be condoned, yet the door would not be slammed shut on a person who was struggling with this problem. There must be acceptance—acceptance of the person not the sin. I would express an open-mindedness to minister to people involved in sin, emphasizing such matters would be dealt with in the context of forgiveness, confidentiality and hope.

Then, secondly, it would be necessary to make it clear that counseling is available. I have only preached one sermon that dealt with homosexuality in our church, and it was four or five months later that a young man made an appointment with me and said, "You remember when you preached that sermon? Well, you talked about my problem in that sermon. You said that our church had a ministry to people who had this particular problem." In this way that brother broke the ice and shared with me his struggle with homosexuality. That was a start for him and for me.

The third step is structuring a direct ministry for those wanting help in turning from the gay life. This might be in the form of a small group fellowship or Bible study. This, in fact, was my approach. It has proved, over three years, to be very effective. In addition, there could be an actual evangelistic extension of church ministry to the gay community. We printed up small posters that were taken from the jacket of the book *The Third Sex?* We then went to the gay bars and asked permission to tack a poster up on the bulletin board. This is one way. I heard of a minister who put an ad in the local newspaper that inferred there was a ministry available to people struggling with the problem of homosexuality. The result was an overwhelming flood of letters asking for help. I wouldn't necessarily advise this kind of approach unless there was really a strong program already developed into which these people could be brought. For example, if we put an ad in the *San Francisco Chronicle* that we had a Christian ministry to homosexuals, we would probably have more people than could be accommodated. We are not in a place in our own ministry where we could ever think of doing anything as dramatic as that. But if a large ministry were developed with a number of counselors and ministers, trained and equipped in this area, an extension to the gay community would bring a large response.

Let me say at this point that the problem of homosexuality is not going to disappear. The numbers of people becoming homosexual is staggering. Our church ministry has always centered around young people. I remember five years ago we never thought about homosexuality in high schools. Not only is it in the high schools, it is now in the junior high schools. It is a problem that is not going to go away. It is growing and I believe that in the near future the problem of homosexuality is going to be much larger than the drug problem, larger in numbers but much more serious as well. I believe homosexuality could become the major problem confronting the church in the years to come. There is a great problem now, and there is great danger that the church will turn away from its responsibility.

You know I love the church, and I am hoping no one will think that I am against the church. I have been ministering for ten years and I know that the church is the only hope for an effective ministry to the homosexual. But we have a challenge here that we cannot ignore. We must deal with this; it is not going to go away. If we are going to follow Jesus Christ, if we are going to preach the gospel to the poor, the oppressed and the captive, we must preach it to the homosexual as well.

Let me express a caution. Ministry to homosexuals is difficult. It is not impossible, but it is a hard ministry and I would say very clearly that it will be costly. Homosexuals, as the rest of us sinners, are notoriously rebellious people. They will rebel against your authority, they will rebel against your straightness, they will rebel against you in any way they possibly can. It will be difficult ministry all the way and you must count the cost. You may lose people out of your fellowship when you begin to minister in this area. It is a costly ministry in terms of time, in terms of patience, in terms of love. It costs in ways that I can't possibly put together at this point. But the cost must indeed be counted and expected.

Now let me describe our program, Love in Action. The format is extremely simple. We meet one evening a week. One week is Bible study with sharing and prayer, the next week is social with a dinner out. Alternating in this way gives a good balance. The Bible study is short and relates to Christian growth. We discuss how we can help the people who write to us. Then we have a time of sharing.

Our group is basically small. We have approximately a dozen core people. Each person has an opportunity to share whatever he would like to. People openly discuss the temptations and problems they face, and bring up questions. Real needs are expressed and prayed about. The meeting lasts between two and three hours during which there are prayer requests for particular needs. At the end we stand together, join hands, and pray over each one of the requests that have emerged during the meeting.

As I said, it is a simple format. In our Love in Action ministry three people take the lead in ministering, myself and two people who have come out of homosexuality and have been free for a number of years. They are solid, mature Christians.

The social gathering is different. One of the girls usually brings a guitar and we sing. There is a time of sharing and of prayer at the end, but our basic purpose is to be together and fellowhsip.

The people who constitute our group do not all come from our church. Many of them, actually most of them, are from other churches, which we feel creates the problem of not being able to provide a total ministry to these people. I don't feel that I have the freedom to minister in a very thorough way to those who are not members of our church because I am not their spiritual authority. This circumstance has presented various kinds of problems over the last couple of years, but in the main the ministry has been functionable. It is possible to have an inter-denominational kind of group, although I prefer to have the members of the group belonging to our own church. I think it is more efficient. You know more of what is going on in their lives if they are a part of your church and you have a greater degree of freedom in helping them to deal with their problems. In other words, if I had to do this over I believe I would like to have made it simply a one-church operation rather than an interdenominational kind of outreach.

Some of the problems that we have experienced have been that people will act out in a rebellious way and seriously disrupt the group. Not having recognized spiritual authority hampers any sort of discipline. I expressed earlier that homosexuality has rebellion at its core. And that rebellious nature is often expressed in meetings. We have actually had a split in our Love in Action group when several people decided they would no longer be a part of our group. I saw it as an act of rebellion. The main issue was whether it was acceptable to "camp," that is, let the homosexual mannerisms and affectations be expressed in the meeting. The leadership disagreed with it, so some members moved off on their own. There will be that kind of rebellion expressed. Probably that is the key problem.

In closing I would like to relate a passage of Scripture that has been important in my life. This is Luke 4:18-19. Jesus was in a synagogue at Nazareth, He was given the Book of the prophet Isaiah, and He read this:

> The Spirit of the Lord is upon me,
> because he has anointed me to
> preach good news to the poor.
> He has sent me to proclaim release
> to the captives
> and recovering of sight to the blind,
> to set at liberty those who are
> oppressed,
> to proclaim the acceptable year of the Lord.

This becomes our ministry as well. He says He was appointed to preach good news to the poor. The homosexual solidly fits into this category, since every homosexual is poor in the kind of good human relationships everyone needs. Jesus said He was sent to proclaim release to the captives. There is nothing more imprisoning, there is no more awful slavery, than homosexuality. Jesus has come to proclaim release to the homosexual. The homosexual is lonely; he has isolated himself, and Jesus has come to bring him love. He came to set at liberty those who are oppressed. Probably the most oppressed subculture in our society is the homosexual. He is oppressed emotionally, spiritually, socially and sexually. And Jesus has come to set at liberty those who are oppressed. That is the gospel. We have the gospel, the church has the gospel. We have it to spread, to share and to proclaim. It is our wonderful privilege, it is also our responsibility. My hope is that the church will minister to those who are trapped in the sin of homosexuality.

7
An Examination of Gay Theology

"Does the Bible prohibit homosexuality?" is the question being asked today as a result of the pro-gay forces operating in the "religious" arena. Gay theology is growing in both stature and sophistication. Bible-centered Christians must be ready to meet the challenge posed by those who are attempting to biblically normalize their transgression. In this chapter I want to examine the major arguments they would use in the attempt to prove that homosexuality is scripturally acceptable.

The first argument is that the Old Testament prohibitions against homosexuality are there so that Israel's population would not be limited. Widespread homosexuality would, of course, serve to reduce the size of the nation. Rather than being moral law, the injunctions against homosexuality are said to be pragmatic; thus, it is reasoned, they are not applicable to us since we are not concerned with increasing the population. On the converse, too, homosexuality might be viewed as preferable to heterosexuality when the number of earthly inhabitants needs to be reduced. If that were so, we would find reference to it in the Old Testament. We can be assured that good exegesis, good interpretation of Scripture, must not be based on silence. In other words, if the Israelites, and God in particular, had been concerned with increasing the population of Israel, we would find evidence to that effect. But we do not. There isn't one single statement along that line in the Bible. The prohibition on homosexuality is based on God's holiness. God is a God of justice and righteousness.

In Genesis, the nature of the creation is obvious, male and female. He created us. In the third chapter of Genesis we see that God joined Adam to Eve. The heterosexual marital relationship comes from the will of God. Violation of that will is basic sin. Since God is holy, homosexuality is judged as unholy. He judges adultery for that reason. It is interesting that the seventh commandment, "Thou shalt not commit adultery" is in the Scripture. If the argument under discussion were true, we would not find the seventh commandment. If people were allowed to have sexual relationships with people other than their spouses, then, of course, the population would be that much greater. Also, we wouldn't find Israel entering into so many wars. When the children of Israel entered the promised land, there were seven nations they engaged in war under God's direction. We would not have this occurrence if God was simply concerned about the size of the nation. No, it is fruitless reasoning that the

114

prohibitions against homosexuality are based on the survival of the people.

A second argument surrounds the prohibitions against homosexuality in Leviticus 18:22 and 20:13. They read:

> You shall not lie with a male as with a woman; it is an abomination.
> If a man lies with a male as with a woman, both of them have committed an abomination; they shall be put to death, their blood is upon them.

Gay theologians say that these prohibitions against homosexuality are for God's special ministers, the priests, and have nothing to do with common man. If this argument were to be admitted, then, of course, it would be assumed that homosexuality would be acceptable for most of the people. However, we need to take a look at the context in which we find these laws. To do that we must examine the first two verses in Leviticus 18. "And the LORD said to Moses, 'Say to the people of Israel, I am the LORD your God.' " The prohibitions against homosexuality are clearly addressed to the entire nation and not simply the priestly class. The context of the passage easily destroys the rationale of the gay theologian. It is impossible to conclude that the commands concerning homosexuality apply only to the priests, for this conclusion has no basis in fact. This can be further demonstrated by examining other verses in Leviticus 18. For example, verse 23, the verse that immediately follows the law about homosexuality reads, "And you shall not lie with any beast and defile yourself with it, neither shall any woman give herself to a beast to lie with it: it is perversion." If we were to say that the prohibitions against homosexuality were simply to the priestly class, why do we find this verse? For one thing, women could not be priests. So it is obvious that the writer inspired by God is not addressing only the priests. We cannot assume that people who were not priests were permitted to have sexual relations with animals. Also, verse 20 of the same chapter of Leviticus says, "And you shall not lie carnally with your neighbor's wife, and defile yourself with her." This prohibition against adultery was to all the people and not simply to the priestly class. No, I think it is quite obvious that in the very clear context of the Scripture, the prohibitions against homosexuality are addressed to all of the people.

This next argument is one of the most interesting put forth by the pro-gay forces. It is more of an emotional appeal than a theological or scriptural disputation. It has to do with the other prohibitions we find in the law, such as the regulations concerning the eating of certain foods. It is one of the more common arguments to be advanced by gay theologians today. It is not a scriptural nor theological rationale at all. It is the old cry of "hypocrites" in the church. A gay theologian, thus, might charge, "How can you Christians enforce the laws against homosexuality when you do not obey those against eating rabbits, oysters, shrimp, and other dietary regulations we find in the Old Testament?" This is every interesting indeed.

I don't see that this point of view weakens the interdicts against homosexuality. For example, if in our church, and it is not difficult to find sinners in our church, I find somebody who is covetous, I am not then given a license to sin in the same way. If some of the Israelites of Moses' day became hungry, found themselves a rabbit and ate it, does that mean that all of the other laws are to be ignored because there was a hypocrite in the camp? We can see the emotional and irrational character of this argument. However, I find a significant, qualitative distinction existing between the moral commands and the dietary and ceremonial rules. Among the Israelites it was one thing to eat a forbidden food and quite another to commit homosexual sin. We see this most clearly in the penalities for breaking the commands. For instance, if an Israelite ate a rabbit, an oyster, or a shrimp, they were to be declared unclean for ceremonial purposes. That's all! However, the penalty for homosexuality was death. The penalties between these two draw our attention to the statement that I made earlier: that is, there is a qualitative distinction between the moral commands and the ceremonial and dietary regulations. Many of the laws that applied to the old covenant of the law ended with the new covenant, when the Lord Jesus Christ broke into history. A glance at any Bible demonstrates that the Old Testament is differentiated from the New Testament. Testament means covenant, it means agreement, it means contract. We have the old covenant and we have the new covenant. Many of the things that applied under the old covenant, particularly regarding ceremonial purity, sacrifice and dietary instructions, were relevant to the old covenant but are not carried over into the new. For instance, the only dietary rule we see in the New Testament is that it would be improper to eat meat that has the blood in it. Also, Paul talked about not offending a weaker brother by eating meat sacrificed to idols. But as to regulations regarding rabbit, oyster and shrimp, we don't find any of these in the New Testament at all. However, we do see the carrying over of the basic moral commands of the Old Testament into the New Testament. "You shall not commit adultery," is the seventh commandment in the Law, but we see Jesus quoting this very command. He said: "Do not commit adultery" (Luke 18:20). The prohibitions against homosexuality in the Old Testament are the same prohibitions in the New Testament. We see it in Romans 1:26-27 and 1 Corinthians 6:9. But we don't find Paul, Jesus, John, Luke, Mark, or Matthew saying anything about eating rabbit, oyster, or shrimp. We see a tremendous difference in the moral command and the dietary regulation. To bring this out just one point further, the law would not allow anyone to minister before God who was lame, blind, or in any way handicapped. However, in the New Testament, we find absolutely no such restriction.

Another argument often used by the gay theologian is based on the story of Sodom and Gomorrah in Genesis 19. Gay theologians contend that the sin for which these cities were destroyed was inhospitality and not homosexuality. It is difficult to see how this conclusion could be drawn from the text, since the implications of homosexual conduct are clear. In the New Testament, references to homosexual practice as being the sin of Sodom and Gomorrah are made in 2 Peter and the letter of Jude. But even if it could be

118

successfully maintained that the contemporary Christian understanding of Genesis 19 is mistaken (which would, in my view, be difficult), it would leave unaffected the unambiguous witness of both the Old and the New Testament that homosexual conduct is against God's will for His people.

Gay theologians delight in fanciful matchmaking. David and Jonathan, for instance, are said to have been homosexual lovers. Paul and Timothy, Ruth and Naomi, Peter and John, and other innocents are accused of engaging in homosexuality. Again, this is presumptuous since it is an argument from silence and inference. There is absolutely nothing solid in Scripture to substantiate such claims.

David and Jonathan, though both were married, are most commonly charged with being gay lovers. Four verses are particularly used. They are:

> The soul of Jonathan was knit to the soul of David, and Jonathan loved him as his own soul. (1 Samuel 18:1)
> Then Jonathan made a covenant with David, because he loved him as his own soul. (1 Samuel 18:3)
> Jonathan, Saul's son, delighted much in David. (1 Samuel 19:1)
> I am distressed for you, my brother Jonathan; very pleasant have you been to me; your love to me was wonderful, passing the love of women. (2 Samuel 1:26)

This is the story of a very close and intimate friendship. There is no reason to believe that sexual love was meant here. Their hearts had been knit together by God. They shared deeply a confidence in one another that David had never experienced, even in marriage. God had brought them together as friends. Their souls, not bodies, were united. Gay theologians must assume (especially in regard to 2 Samuel 1:26) that all love is sexual. Jonathan and David could share deep love together without there being anything sexual about it. The most telling point, though, is that if they had a homosexual relationship it would have caused such a stir and created such a landmark precedent, commentary on it would have appeared often in Scripture.

A powerful issue for the gay theologian involves the fact that Jesus and the Gospel writers, Matthew, Mark, Luke, and John, did not even mention homosexuality in their writings.

This is true, they don't. Jesus did not talk about homosexuality at all. Let me pose this question, however. Is it to be assumed that since Jesus did not declare homosexuality to be a sin, that it is not a sin? Of course not! Jesus had no need to say anything about homosexuality. The Jews, particularly in Judea, were very anti-homosexual. Jesus certainly knew about homosexuality, but it was not a question that He had to deal with. Jesus and the evangelists, Matthew, Mark, Luke, and John, assumed and accepted the Old Testament teaching on sex. Sex outside of marriage was sin. They assumed that position and had no need to actually confront the problem of homosexuality.

Homosexuality did exist in the world in which Jesus lived. For a period of time it was popular in Greece as we observe in any history of the decline of the Greek culture. It was looked to as something above customary heterosexuality. But the Jews did not tolerate it. I remember reading in one pro-gay newsletter that Jesus probably picked one of His disciples to be a homosexual partner. This argument has absolutely no merit whatsoever. Jesus traveled with a band of people. The Pharisees, the Sadducees, the scribes, the people of the established religious institutions swarmed around Jesus. They watched Him and they questioned Him. If they could have gotten anything on Him, they would have used it to the full extent. If they had at all suspected, even for a moment, with the slightest kind of evidence, that Jesus was involved in any sort of homosexuality, they would have used it with glee. They would have discredited Him, and very probably would have killed Him for it. Homosexuality in the first century was a capital offense among the Jews. Recall the time a woman caught in adultery was brought before Jesus (John 8). The religious leaders were ready to stone her. If they had found somebody caught in the act of homosexuality, the punishment would have been the same. In the day that Jesus lived, homosexuality was not at all tolerated. Even though Jesus and the Gospel writers did not mention homosexuality, there was no need to.

Paul comes under repeated attack from supporters of a homosexual life style. There are two pertinent passages. The first is 1 Corinthians 6:9-10.

> Do you not know that the unrighteous will not inherit the kingdom of God? Do not be deceived; neither the immoral, nor idolaters, nor adulterers, nor homosexuals, nor thieves, nor the greedy, nor drunkards, nor revilers, nor robbers will inherit the kingdom of God.

121

Gay theologians maintain that in this passage Paul wasn't putting down homosexuality and declaring it a sin, but was merely inferring that there should be no sin in homosexual relationships. This argument is fairly easily dealt with. For example, Paul mentions idolaters. Shouldn't the same consideration extend to idolaters? In other words, you shouldn't let any sin enter into your idolatry. Now that is ludicrous because *all* idolatry is sin, not merely some of it. And the same can be said for every other type of sin that Paul mentions. The Bible doesn't hedge at all. Our approach to Scripture must be honest. The word homosexual is specifically mentioned and it is very clearly presented that a homosexual will not enter into the kingdom of God, not only those who have "sinful" homosexual relationships. The truth is that all homosexual relationships are sinful. It is impossible to say that homosexuality is good as long as it isn't lustful. There is no such thing as good, clean, healthy, loving, non-sinful homosexuality. All homosexuality is immoral and illicit, as is all adultery, fornication, drunkenness, idolatry, thievery, and robbery.

In addition, it is sometimes maintained that Paul's words translated in the Revised Standard Version "homosexuals" and in the King James Version, "effeminate" do not mean homosexuality at all. Let us examine the words. There are two words in the Greek text that together yield "homosexuals." The first is the word *malakoi*. This refers to persons who allow themselves to be misused homosexually. The second word is *arsenokoitai*. This is a word used to describe a male homosexual. Both of these words refer clearly and explicitly to homosexuality.

The second disputed Pauline passage is Romans 1:26-27. It has been argued that Paul is not specifically dealing with homosexuality. It is true that Paul is not solely addressing the subject of homosexuality. In the broader context he is dealing with man's rebellion against God. Paul is concerned with the process of what happens to man when he begins to turn away from God. But to say that Paul is not centering on the question of homosexuality does not mean that the passage can be simply thrown out. Such a consideration has nothing to do with the rightness or wrongness of what Paul said. He wrote that, because of the rebellion of men,

> ... God gave them up to dishonorable passions. Their women exchanged natural relations for unnatural, and the men likewise gave up natural relations with women and were consumed with passion for one another, men committing shameless acts with men and receiving in their own persons the due penalty of their error.

Paul definitely identifies homosexuality. He is using homosexuality as an illustration of man's rebellion against God. He certainly sees homosexuality as a grievous sin comparable to idolatry (verses 24-25).

It has also been argued that Paul was addressing a Roman situation, and previously a Corinthian circumstance, both instances too unlike our own day to be applicable. In other words, Paul's statements about homosexuality in Romans and 1 Corinthians are culturally bound, that is, they are not relevant to today's society. I think it is recognizable that all men, regardless of epic, era, language, race, religion, or culture, are all basically the same. We have the same needs, problems, desires and sins. Cross-culturally, the nature of man is one. This argument does not stand up. There is no reason why such an argument should be accepted. Paul's writing cannot be dismissed by saying they are irrelevant. If it were true that Paul's discussion on homosexuality was irrelevant, what about his statements about murder, lying, or adultery? Are they not applicable in our culture as well? Yes, they are as suitable as his statements about homosexuality. Paul knew about homosexuality. And in his statements against it he well knew what he was dealing with.

Using the "culturally bound" concept to dismiss Paul exposes a deficient view of the Bible. If the Scripture is not inspired by God, why worry about what it says at all? Honestly dealing with the Bible demands an acceptance of all the Bible, not simply the passages we agree with.

Proponents of gay theology will point out that today's churches are inconsistent in regard to such Pauline commands as those concerning women keeping silent in church and the wearing of hats. This argument reminds us of the rabbit, oyster, and shrimp controversy of the Old Testament. However, it does challenge the relevance of Paul's statement in Romans and in 1 Corinthians. In other words, because Paul wrote of homosexuality and also dealt with other issues, and since many churches today do not practice these, the question is, "Why do they keep the commands of Romans 1 and 1 Corinthians 6?" If all of the churches ignored the instructions about hats, veils, and women's silence, this does not nullify the clear testimony that homosexuality is sin. The accusation of hypocrisy, justified or not, does not suddenly make homosexuality acceptable. Some churches do strictly observe regulations such as women wearing hats in church meetings, while others, ignoring the letter of the law, keep the principles. However, moral commandments are not at all situational or cultural. It may be argued that the wearing of hats by women in today's churches is irrelevant. But you won't find the same thinking associated with murder, rape and adultery. These are moral commandments as are the prohibitions against homosexuality. They stand without qualification for every culture and every period of history.

Some gay theologians attempt to remove homosexuality from any ethical context. This is the third sex dispute. Such an approach infers that homosexuality is genetic in origin, and thus one cannot speak of homosexuality's rightness or wrongness. Many gay Christians are proud of their gayness and refer to it as a gift from God. They may even view it as a cross they are to bear. In the extreme, they may use their gayness as a platform to witness to the grace of God. It is the converse of "the devil made me do it," rationale and becomes "God made me do it."

We cannot biblically say "God made me do it" and we cannot, on the other hand, believe "the devil made me do it." The position that God makes someone homosexual simply has no biblical support. For example, there is murder, a sin likened to homosexuality. Can a murderer protest, "God made me a murderer"? If that were so, the Bible would say,

"Thou shalt commit murder." Or a greedy person might say, "I am naturally a covetous person, it is in my genes, that's the way I am. God made me a covetous person. My covetousness is not a sin, rather it is something God gave me that I have to deal with and bear." If that were true, God would not say, "Thou shalt not covet." If God gave anybody homosexuality as a gift, or as a cross to bear, there would be no commandments against homosexuality. In Scripture we clearly see there is a rightness and a wrongness in regard to sexuality. There is no third sex.

Another point of argumentation is that the Bible is only against lustful homosexuality, not homosexuality as such. In this regard, Romans 14:14 is often quoted. "I know and am persuaded in the Lord Jesus that nothing is unclean in itself; but it is unclean for any one who thinks it unclean." In this verse, it is supposed that Paul declares everything to be clean. If nothing is unclean in itself, then homosexuality without lust is clean and right. However, this is to ignore the obvious context of the passage. In reading the opening verses of chapter 14, you will see that Paul is addressing himself to the questions of food and religious holidays. Probably the food in question is food offered to idols and the days may be in regard to disputations concerning the proper day for assembling to worship. He is not dealing with any moral or ethical commands, and he is definitely not overthrowing all of Moses' and Jesus' commandments about sin. When the gay Christian, therefore, uses Romans 14:14 as an argument that permits homosexuality without lust, he is ignoring the context of the passage. To reemphasize this point, we cannot speak of clean adultery and

126

unclean adultery, clean hatred and unclean hatred, or clean homosexuality and unclean homosexuality. They are *all* unclean by nature of what they are.

Finally I would like to address the misuse of the law of love. It is understandable that the homosexual would desire to see homosexuality covered under the broad classification of love. And since the Bible says that "God is love" and "love covers a multitude of sins," homosexuality, an expression of "love," must be legitimate. However, love is ethical. Love depends on integrity and sound morality. That which deviates from integrity and biblical morality cannot be love. A person may love a painting, but when that person covets the painting so much he plans to steal it, love has been perverted. In a relationship between two men or two women where there is friendship, understanding, concern and compassion, if that relationship becomes a physical, sexual thing, real love is gone. For example, the love that David and Jonathan shared was a pure love. If they had entered into a sexual relationship, then the love would have gone beyond the bounds of morality and biblical injunction and would have become transgression.

God loves me, but as a loving heavenly Father, He lets me know through His Word and my conscience that stealing, for instance, is a sin. And it is actually due to love that God points these things out to us. Many homosexuals think that since God prohibits homosexuality He cannot be a God of love. We see, though, that when God commands, when He reveals His will, it is for our good because He loves us. God prohibits homosexuality because He loves us; it is not His plan for us.

The Bible says, "Male and female He created them." God made us male and female and He gave Eve to Adam in marriage. We see no hint of homosexuality in the accounts of the creation at all. So then, when God prohibits homosexuality He preserves the natural order of the creation. Homosexuality is unnatural, it is against the creation of God. We do the Scripture and God's nature a great injustice when we cover over the sin of homosexuality by saying it is all love. In my growing up as a Christian, I have encountered a number of things in the Scriptures that I reacted against. I would search for a theological out, a rationale for getting around troublesome laws and principles. But I had to realize that it was an attitude of unrepentance on *my* part that made me desire to nullify God's Word. We must be concerned about a right relationship with God more than manipulating passages that challenge our thinking and living.

8
Homophobia and Misogamy

At eight years of age he and a neighbor boy had played "doctor" a few times. Now a friend was openly practicing homosexuality, and other friends were talking about a gay film they had seen in San Francisco. He had failed at various girlfriend-boyfriend relationships. Occasionally there were fantasies involving homosexuality. He had it, homophobia—the fear of being homosexual.

She was one of fourteen girls in the office. At lunch they would sometimes talk of their boyfriends. Lately a few girls sat apart and talked. Word got around about them—gay! She watched it grow until there were four, finally six. Nearly half the office staff had turned gay. She was afraid she'd be next. Another victim of homophobia.

She had been with three, four, maybe five boys that month, and she couldn't figure out which might be the father. Why all the promiscuity? The parents seemed stable and responsible. The girl was not the rebellious type and did well in school. Months later she found the courage to say it. She wanted to prove she wasn't gay.

With the tremendous growth in homosexuality (some observers estimate the homosexual population is 20 million in America) and, even more importantly, the news media's extended coverage of the pro-gay forces, homophobia, the fear of being homosexual, is growing. Gay liberation groups are hoping to first gain acceptance for homosexuality from society, and secondly, see homosexuality normalized. They essentially want the homosexual life style to be as approved of as is the heterosexual. This means having homosexuality presented in our educational institutions, at all levels, as desirable and normal. The laws of our land do not seem able to withstand the attack. The social contact, seemingly society's only social ethic, is in a constant state of flux.

Homophobia thrives in such an atmosphere. Young men and women, even older men and women, are vulnerable to this fear.

In addition we have experienced a sexual revolution in recent years. Our moral standards have been seriously damaged. Sexual immorality is commonplace, accepted, even approved of by large segments of our society. People who have been, knowingly or unknowingly, affected by this distorted moral climate have suffered great harm in terms of their sexual identity. Sin characteristically robs a person of security and maturity. Those then who are confused about their sexuality will be more vulnerable to homophobia than those who have obeyed God's principles.

Paranoia, a type or degree of fear, is a dangerous state of mind. It produces increased instability and emotionally paralyzes a person. Individuals can succumb to the very thing they fear; one way to escape the fear is to give in to it.

This process occurred with a young man who came to me for counsel. In elementary school, perhaps due to his small stature or his unwillingness to engage in playground sports, the other kids poked fun at him. He felt friendless and different. As far as I know, his home was good; he never expressed any resentment or bitterness towards his parents, though I probed that area. An older brother and his father spent much of their leisure time working on cars and motorcycles. As he showed a similar interest in mechanics his father and brother drew him into their hobby. Repairing, refining and driving machines became a major source of entertainment and helped him establish an identity.

Despite the relationship with his family, the rest of the world (in his eyes at least) was not accepting of him. There grew in him an abnormal need for acceptance. He lacked confidence with almost everyone outside of the family. As a high school student he felt lonely and unattractive to others. He said people treated him differently.

During his last year of high school he became acquainted with a few other boys who were also on the social fringe. Though these friends didn't share his interest in cars, they accepted him. As the months wore on, these friends became more and more important to him. That summer, on a camp-out, he found his friends to be homosexual. The episode frightened him to the point that he dropped out of the group.

Now, however, he would wonder about himself. A fear grew that he was different too.

He put in long hours at the library reading everything he could about homosexuality. Gradually he lost interest in everything but this one question—was he a homosexual too? Loneliness closed in on him as well; he was afraid of everyone. He was different, he knew, but was he a homosexual? Homophobia troubled him for five long years.

Family members tried to talk to him but to no avail. Only he knew what the problem really was. The tension was severe and, regardless of the diversions he sought, he was never entirely free from the homophobia.

Through a job contact he met a man who was obviously homosexual. There was a repulsion and an attraction at the same time. A friendship was established and new friends were made. Eventually, over a period of many months, my counselee tried homosexuality.

In our talks I established that he was not exclusively attracted sexually to men. His fantasies were most often of women. I could not find indications of genuine homosexuality; he did not prefer men to women though he had never had sexual relations with a woman. There was the fear, the homophobia. There was also the need for acceptance. He was not homosexual in reality. The fear so dominated his life he gave in to homosexuality to escape it. After that point was established in the counseling he recognized he was heterosexual, he accepted it, and did definitely reject homosexuality.

How might homophobia be dealt with? How can we as Christians help a person work through a homophobic reaction?

First of all, let me say that only the gospel can bring genuine wholeness to a person suffering from homophobia. In many non-Christian approaches to the problem, acceptance is the key word. The idea is that anxiety and fear will be reduced when one accepts the homosexuality. It is almost that if you fear you are homosexual then you are, so stop fighting it and be what you fear you are. This thinking is faulty, of course. We know from the Scriptures that fear is to be rejected, not received. In the salvation message, we have all the tools necessary to meet the challenge homophobia presents.

It is essential to establish what homosexuality actually is. The definition I am using here has been accepted by EXODUS, a coalition of individuals and groups nationwide who are actively involved in ministry to the homosexual. This definition reads: "Homosexuality is a sexual object choice characterized by an ongoing erotic preference for partners of the same sex."

We observe that this definition is behavioristic-oriented. But, notice the word "choice" and "preference." Real homosexuality involves conscious choice: a decision is made although the gay person is not usually aware of the choice on his part.

Preference does not exclude the possibility of homosexual fantasies. A person who has been involved in homosexual activities at some point, but who prefers the opposite sex, is guilty of committing the sin of homosexuality, but is not a homosexual. In addition, the word "ongoing" is used. This means that a person who is qualified, according to our definition, as a homosexual at one point, may at another point be classed not a homosexual. It is my feeling that many people are needlessly worried about their sexual identity. After some examination I have often found that people who fear they are homosexual are in fact not so at all. There may be a sexual battle going on inside but the person is not necessarily homosexual.

An important point in dealing with any fear is to admit its presence. Fear is often stripped of its power when it can be examined and prayed about. The vague, nebulous fears are the ones that torment us the most. When a person can identify the problem—"I'm afraid I'm a homosexual"—he is on his was to reducing that fear. And when we know what we are up against and are able to talk about it, ventilation can occur which helps alleviate frustration.

Fear may actually be a sin. In the Bible we find ". . . God hath not given us a spirit of fear; but of power, and of love, and of a sound mind" (2 Timothy 1:7, KJV). If God has not given it, then it is sin, and we do not have to submit to it. Paul wrote, ". . . ye have not received the spirit of bondage again to fear; but ye have received the Spirit of adoption, whereby we cry, Abba, Father" (Romans 8:15 KJV). Fear will not be able to stand in the presence of God's love. The Spirit of adoption is the Spirit of love, the Holy Spirit. Since God loves us and has brought us into His family, we have perfect security and protection from fear as we abide in that love.

Another point in dealing with homophobia is the

accepting of God's evaluation of homosexuality. God's word provides security, even in its prohibitions. Important passages along this line are: Genesis 1:27-28, 2:24, 5:1-2; Leviticus 18:22, 20:13; Romans 1:26-27; 1 Corinthians 6:9-11; and 1 John 2:15-17. These commandments and principles are there as direction from a loving Father who cares enough to say no. Yielding to the Word of the Lord on homosexuality is a strong defense against homophobia.

Strong walls make a sturdy and secure building. Saying no to homosexual fantasy and temptations help build strong moral walls. I am speaking here of asserting the will over the emotions. Since we are made in the image of God we have the capacity to decide for or against sin. Jesus' story of the wise man who built his house on the rock and the foolish man who built his house on the sand applies. Jesus is our rock where temptations and sins fall impotently aside. The emotions that would lead us into dangerous places, i.e., dissatisfaction, loneliness, despair, discouragement, can be withstood. Every temptation can be viewed then as an instrument whereby the will can be strengthened and a victory won.

The mercy of God is powerful in its effect. People suffering from homophobia can be obsessed with guilt and condemnation especially if they have struggled with it for many years. They do need the confirmation of God's forgiveness. 1 John 1:9 reads, "If we confess our sins, he is faithful and just, and will forgive us our sins and cleanse us from all unrighteousness." We know this was written for Christians who found themselves in need of daily forgiveness. The problem is that guilt so often recurs; perhaps vestiges of it may hold on for years. John realized this and spoke to the problem in 1 John 2:1-2. He is careful to assert that God's will is that we not sin, but adds that if anyone does sin we have help, help in the form of the Advocate, Jesus Christ. Forgiveness is centered in Jesus who has already completely provided for the forgiveness anyone will ever need. Fear is robbed of its power in the light of God's forgiveness and grace.

A last point in coping with homophobia is an acceptance of whom God has made us. Scripture tells us that He has made us male and female (Genesis 1:27). No one is born a homosexual. A true homosexual has accepted something that is totally contrary to reality. A person facing the problem of homophobia can reject that which is false and cling to the truth of whom God has made him. God does not make mistakes and does not change, "For the gifts and the call of God are irrevocable" (Rom. 11:29).

Homophobia may be growing, but the gospel of Christ is an effective standard against it. Personally I have seen that homophobia is not overly difficult to deal with once it is identified. Christ-centeredness does help establish a secure sexual identity. Homophobia is one of those enemies that runs at the approach of God's army.

Misogamy is a problem which is sometimes mistaken as either homosexuality or homophobia. It may be so confused by either the person suffering from it or by someone observing it in another person.

The 1973 edition of *The Random House Dictionary* says that misogamy is "the hatred of marriage." *Taber's Cyclopedic Medical Dictionary* says it is "aversion to marriage." Misogamy must not be confused with misogyny, which is the abnormal hatred of women. And being single does not make one a misogamist.

I would like to expand the above definition of misogamy to include the following: misogamy, in addition to hatred of marriage, is the extreme fear or mistrust of members of the opposite sex to the extent that marriage would seem an impossibility.

A misogamist fears any intimate or committed (often sexual) contact with the opposite sex. He is not a homosexual, though it is conceivable he could become one. There have been several homosexuals I have counseled who were misogamists with significant predisposition toward homosexuality and eventually did become homosexual. It is probable that most misogamists are confirmed heterosexuals and would not be tempted toward homosexuality at all. However, a misogamist might ignorantly suppose himself to be homosexual as he tries to analyze why he fears the opposite sex.

A misogamist may fall prey to homophobia. If, in trying to come to grips with his problem regarding the opposite sex, he hits upon homosexuality as the answer, a homophobia reaction may result. A true misogamist knows, though, that he is not homosexual. He may be easily sexually aroused by the opposite sex and engage in sexual activity with others of the opposite sex. Sex for a misogamist tends to be impersonal, businesslike, uncommitted, and primarily biological.

Dealing with misogamy is relatively new to me personally. One year ago I'd never heard the word. But in counseling people in the Love in Action ministry to homosexuals, I began encountering people with homophobia and misogamy. Initially I did not recognize the fear of marriage for what it was. And at first I thought that it wasn't a real problem. My initial reaction was, "Well, good, you are not homosexual." I never thought of helping the person. However, after some research into that area, I began to see the severity of the problem and the need to minister to it. Also, the great numbers of people suffering from misogamy have become more evident to me. It seems possible that misogamy is more prevalent than either homophobia or homosexuality. Now I can recognize misogamy and try to bring some help. This has been important since most misogamists do not recognize this problem in themselves.

Misogamy is not a pretty word. It sounds like an awful, even evil, disease. In my mind it is not a sin; but it is, of course, a result of sin. This would be social sin or the influence of sin from family and parents, the social environment, or the product of wrong choices. Parents can instill a fear of marriage in their children in ways we are all familiar with: drug abuse, alcoholism, sexual perversion (e.g., adultery or incest), fear and hatred in the home, and many others. People who have been severely injured through sexual promiscuity, divorce, severe rejection by the opposite sex, and those who have very low self-esteem and confidence in themselves may be candidates for misogamy. Girls who have been raped, molested, or wrongfully used by men can come to hate and fear them. People who have been continually wounded through repeated failures with the opposite sex may have trouble with misogamy.

The causes and predisposing factors are certainly far more complex and varied than I have just described. This is a new area for me, but the following brief description of persons who have personally experienced misogamy may help bring the matter into perspective.

Sue, in her early thirties, had been divorced for two years after seven years of marriage. She immediately (on the rebound) entered into another relationship from which she was eventually forced to flee. She wanted no other men in her life. They had rejected her twice, involved her in complex and frustrating legal and personal entanglements, and her two boys were starting to have trouble in school. Misogamy was the result. Homosexuality or homophobia were not involved. Sue decided celibacy was the course for her.

Jim, never married and in his early thirties, was frightened of women. He occasionally dated but did it simply to keep up appearances. Well-educated and with a good job, he was a handsome man, athletically inclined. There seemed to be two problems. One was a very poor self-image. He was beginning to bald but, to me at least, this mattered little in his overall appearance. Two, he did not want to lose his freedom. Marriage to Jim meant shackles of iron. He owned a sports car, traveled a great deal, played tennis and golf, and he wanted nothing to interfere. Sex was not a significant factor in his life, either.

Bill had been married several times. Finally with the fourth wife he began to search for an answer. He could not perform sexually. Thousands of dollars poured into every imaginable therapy brought no relief. After reading a newspaper article he decided he was a misogamist. Although he would marry, he was afraid of sexual involvement with women. Earlier in his life he had tried homosexuality, but one brief halfway encounter convinced him he was not homosexual. The trouble seemed to have stemmed from a very embarrassing failure and rejection when he tried to seduce his teen-age sweetheart. The scars that were left and the guilt and anger turned inward toward women robbed him of the ability to relate sexually to any of his wives.

Liz grew up to feel that sex was dirty. She had observed her mother in sexual encounters with many men for years as a child. Sex was dirty, men were dirty; men did dirty things to her mother. Sex was dirty, but fun. Cheap sex thrills were the only thrills for Liz. This is the way she related to men and sex. After Liz was born again, she lost her sexual identity. She didn't care if she ever married. Sex was only good if it was bad. As a Christian she learned sex was good and beautiful, but only in marriage. With sex stripped of its evilness, Liz was no longer interested.

Paul lived in his head. He would intellectualize everything. He was also fearful of being organic. Sex was therefore out. It wasn't intellectual, and it was certainly quite organic. Kissing was absolutely out of the question. And marriage was just too much trouble. He would say, "How could you lay there and have someone breathing, coughing, moving and sleeping right beside you in the same bed?" Through these attitudes he avoided sex and marriage. Somewhere deep within him he had learned to fear women and any committed relationship with them.

None of these five were homosexual or

homophobic. There were hints at the causes of the misogamy with some but not with others. Variation in circumstances was obvious. However, each one could be termed a misogamist.

A homosexual must see that homosexuality is sinful, be willing to turn from it, and receive ministry aimed at building him up in his new life. A homophobic, through various sorts of ministry, can learn to verbalize his fear, give it up to God, accept that truth about himself, and then grow out of his fear with biblical confidence.

Misogamy is treated somewhat the same way as homophobia is. Both involve the recognizing of fear, the positive motion of reducing that fear, and an acceptance of basic biblical truths.

My particular means of ministry to misogamists follows a rather loose or disjointed process that includes these aspects. One, I have a person ask himself, "Why am I single?" This question over a period of time may lead to the reasons for the fear or at least cause recognition that some sort of fear is involved. Two, I bring people with the same problem into a discussion group. This calls for an investment and calls for a definite commitment to deal with the fear. Feedback from others is very helpful too. It is comforting to know someone else is faced with something similar. Three, I encourage ventilation or a verbalizing of the fear before others. This helps to reduce fear. Group encouragement to try dating and to seek out a relationship helps to produce healing. In the group process, a person can learn to relate in a positive way to the opposite sex. Simply seeing that persons of the opposite sex also fear marriage fosters growth. Four, I point out Bible truths which aid in moving a person away from misogamy. The truth that sex in marriage is good and right can be extremely beneficial. Knowing that God made sex can alter unhealthy attitudes toward marriage. The fact that God calls us to relate to one another, that fellowship and communion is normal and uplifted, can assist in a person's reevaluation of personal involvements.

In most of the instances I have seen, misogamy is not an extraordinarily difficult problem to deal with. Any fear exposed to the light and identified loses very much of its power. Ministers of the gospel have a distinct advantage in coping with misogamy. As a person commits himself to a body of believers, the Christ-given warmth and love in the church family is an ideal environment for the healing of misogamy. In the church a person can learn to trust others, value them as children of God, and have freedom to enter into healthy relationships. Besides all this, there is the Holy Spirit who miraculously works to dissolve fear, promote confidence and trust, and bring an experience of love that can overflow to others.

In conclusion, I would say that homosexuality, homophobia, and misogamy would be staggering problems without the power and hope of Jesus Christ and His gospel. The fact that these enigmas can and do become cleared up points to the reality of our God and His love.

9
Love in Action Newsletters

Dear Friends,   December 1975
   This is the first of a series of newsletters that will be
coming your way monthly from our fellowship here in
San Rafael, a group of Christian men and women with
homosexual backgrounds. Our main purpose is to
reach out to other gay people in order to show that it is
possible to deal with the many problems facing
them—from a Christian point of view—by people who
have been through the same things and are still going
through difficult times, but dealing with these burdens
in new strength and victory.
   But I'm getting ahead of my story. Let's go back to
the beginning. Our group began almost two years ago
with Rev. Kent Philpott (not a homosexual) of Church
of the Open Door through his counseling ministry,
headquartered in San Rafael. His book *The Third Sex?*
(Logos) describes the actual beginnings, so I will not go

into it here, except to say that it was through the efforts, concerns and love of this man of God that started an outreach to homosexuals who were willing to find a way out of entrapment. Our core group has remained relatively small, but our contacts with others through letters, tapes, and personal interviews have grown tremendously in two years. Our ministry (recently named Love in Action) reaches out all over the United States, and we see no limits as to what geographic area it will take us, providing that people want to be helped.

My name is Bob and I will be writing and editing the newsletter each month in hopes of discussing some real problems and issues. My own story can be read in Chapter 3 of *The Third Sex?*, and it is not a pretty story, believe me. But my whole life is changing and so will yours, if you're willing to put your faith and trust in Jesus Christ and *know* that He can do it. Take my word for it. Better yet, take *His* Word for it (2 Corinthians 5:17). If you have not yet read *The Third Sex?*, then that should be your first priority. If you cannot get it at a bookstore, then you can get one from us by sending four dollars. Also, if you are interested in tapes dealing with various problems, they are available from us at two dollars each or free-on-loan. There are now six tapes (all men). My own tape, a follow-up of my own story, will be out in late January, and later a tape from Polly (Chap. 4) on some of her thinking. In addition to all this, you may correspond with any of those in our fellowship, male or female. We also offer counseling on an individual basis with Kent or with any of several in our group who will be happy to meet with you.

So you see, we're mainly interested in *you*, at

whatever level you are. If you are super-shy and afraid to come out in the open, we don't blame you. We do want to assure you that you can trust us completely—no names will ever be used. You can start with the book and/or the tapes if you wish, or write any of us. Later, if you are in the area, you can arrange to see one of us in complete privacy. *No* pressures, *no* obligations, just a love outreach to you personally by someone who knows what it's all about. We're not asking for money. The newsletter is free, sent in a sealed envelope each month. The *only* cost is if you wish to buy the book or tapes, but if you are not able, we'll be happy to loan them to you free.

In this first newsletter, I have to say a few important things on behalf of the whole group. I think you need to know exactly what we believe and where we stand scripturally. There is a lot of false teaching about homosexuality and our position needs to be made clear. Certain churches teach gay identity and the Christian life style, side by side, sort of "having your cake and eating it too," as the saying goes. This is a very attractive approach, since it allows you to follow Christ, be a Christian, and participate in homosexual relations. Our ministry believes this to be false and stands on the biblical teaching that such sexual conduct is wrong and against God's teaching. Our basis for this is 1 Corinthians 6:9-10, Romans 1:24-27, and Leviticus 18:22, and is discussed in detail by Kent in his book. We believe it and we stand on that truth, difficult as it might be. In making a positive commitment to Christ, we hold firm the belief that He will lead us through this valley, give us victory over homosexual desires and give us a new life and a new walk that is within his will.

He will do this if it means our remaining single and celibate. This is a costly price for people so highly oriented toward sex, but worth it, if we are to hold our faith up in truth.

Also, we need to make a statement about doctrine. We believe that the Bible is the inspired Word of God and is infallible and authoritative in the original writings. We believe in one God, eternally existent in three Persons: Father, Son, and Holy Spirit. We believe in the deity of our Lord Jesus Christ, in his virgin birth, in His sinless life, in His death and atonement, in His bodily resurrection, in His ascension, and in His personal return. We believe that for the salvation of lost and sinful man, faith in the Lord Jesus Christ and regeneration by the Holy Spirit are essential. We believe in the present ministry of the Holy Spirit, by whose indwelling the Christian is enabled to live a godly life. We believe in the forgiveness of sins, the resurrection of the body, and life eternal. We believe in the spiritual unity of the church, which is the body of Christ, composed of all who are regenerated through faith in the Lord Jesus Christ.

This first newsletter has been rather formal, but was necessary to lay a foundation. Future newsletters will be dealing with specific problems of the gay Christian and homosexuals in general.

Love in Action fellowship is part of House Ministries, an interdenominational, evangelical, Christ-centered ministry that has many forms in the Bay Area. All inquiries should be made to the following address: Love in Action, 2130 Fourth Street, San Rafael, California, 94901.

Have a beautiful and victorious Christmas season. We love you and hold our hand out to each of you in fellowship and concern.

Yours in Christ,
Bob

* * *

Dear Friends,   January 1976

The holiday season is over once again and we can look forward together to a year filled with renewed spirit, strength, and victory through our Lord Jesus Christ. These are the great promises that I am reminded of as I reflect upon the past few weeks of celebration, a special time for all of us as we look ahead to the freedom to be the new people we are in Him. I praise God again for the greatest gift of all, Jesus Christ, Who Himself gave everything that we might live and be set free. Exciting? Realistic? Believable? Most definitely yes on all counts, as we grow in faith together and wait in patience for His exciting will to be done in each of our lives. May your New Year be the brightest ever and rich in His blessings.

Last month, in our first newsletter, we laid the groundwork for our ministry and tried to explain exactly where we stand, both on homosexuality and on Scripture, so we will not pursue that again until the need arises. We plan to send copies of that first newsletter out to each *new* person added to our mailing list, since it is important that our viewpoints are clear to all. Then, later, if questions come up, we will deal with them at that time. We, in Love in Action Fellowship, realize only too well what we are up against in terms of our beliefs as far as the gay community in general is concerned, and the gay church in particular, a growing body. That can be a very alluring and exciting life style to someone who has tasted it, let's not kid ourselves. Unless you've actually been involved, it's impossible to really know what it's all about. But we stand firm on what we believe, at whatever the cost, and look forward to the time when we can deal with all our problems as we grow in Him. We are not afraid of the gay community, because we were a part of it and understand all of its many sides only too well. To us it is a challenge, because it is this very group where our love and concern are focused.

This brings us right up to the problem and its very heart—the attraction to the gay life as opposed to that of the celibate, Jesus-centered Christian homosexual. Really, what are the alternatives? Stating them is the easy part. The hard part is putting the alternative into practice, depending, of course, upon what you choose. They are simple to state in words. You can continue in a homosexual life style, pursuing all the various forms of emotional and physical experiences, exciting times, etc., and in the end, whenever that moment comes, you are spiritually dead, apart from God, destined for eternity in Hell following God's judgment of all mankind. Harsh? Fanatical-sounding? Unreasonable? Yes, but *true*. There is no other way to state it. That is the choice. Are you going to be ready to face it when the moment comes? Of course you won't be, but then it'll be too late. The chance will be gone. A lot of religious hogwash you say? That is the choice you have to make, and the risk is all yours. We've made ours. The joy and peace that is ours, despite the burdens, far surpass anything that we pretend "might have been."

The only other alternative is to choose Jesus Christ

and give up the homosexual life style. That is what we have all done and to us there is no other way. There are no other alternatives. Choosing both Christianity and the gay life is a complete delusion. I know that all of this sounds terribly harsh, cruel and unjust. I know only too well the full implications of what I am saying, but either we are going to obey God's Word or we aren't. There is no middle ground. There is no watered-down, frosted-over version of a spiritual life in Christ that will permit a person to continue in a pattern that is clearly labeled sin. It is ludicrous to think that homosexuality is an exception when the Bible clearly states otherwise. People who choose to see only what they want to see in God's Word are only deluding themselves. I know it's difficult. Perhaps you say it's impossible. Yes, I would agree that it sounds and feels pretty impossible, especially when temptation rears its head right in front of you, which it does frequently. But you have to hang in there and *believe* that nothing is impossible for Him to accomplish in our lives. *We* may not see it, but He can and He *will* change us; but we must learn patience. We must be fully willing, and the commitment must be made strongly and decisively. The "middle-of-the-road" compromise will never bring victory, but only eventual defeat. This is an area of real faith, the core of it that helps us to step out with Him in control.

I have talked about a number of important things this month, some of them quite harsh and rather demanding. I dislike having to talk this way to people because this is what turned me completely off as a young man. It literally made me sour towards religion, even though I never ever lost God completely. So, I apologize if my words sound like hellfire and brimstone preaching. But really, it is so important to get across the idea that we are literally playing with fire in our lives and if we're going to be God's children, then we *have* to say it the way it is. Believe me when I say that love and concern are the very roots of my plea. If I didn't care about you, why should I bother with all this, but I do care. We all do, and we have grown to despise what this life does to people. Your situation might be fantastically beautiful right at this moment, and I certainly don't want to burst anyone's bubble. However, all you have to do is review our lives (*The Third Sex?*) to understand. These are so typical of the pattern as the years creep by. Have you ever really stopped to think what things might be like ten, twenty, thirty years from now? So many gay people live only for today. I know. I certainly did.

In ending this month's letter, I want to say how I hope I haven't put it to you too strongly, but I feel that we need to speak up for what God is saying to us. Next month we are going to talk about masturbation, fantasies, and pitfalls. I will also be reviewing the book *Sons of Freedom*, by Gini Andrews, which has a very interesting chapter entitled "Forever Gay?" Again, have a glorious 1976.

Yours in Christ,
Bob

*   *   *

Dear Friends,   February 1976

This past month has been an exciting time for our fellowship here in San Rafael. We have been blessed with a number of new people that will be connected to our ministry on a personal level. Our core group is growing, and we are thrilled that God is blessing us in this way. As our ministry continues to grow, our outreach to others is extended in many directions and we pray that our Lord will help us to touch many lives in the months and years to come. Also, it is great to receive so many letters from our friends all over the country in response to the newsletter. We consider each of you on our mailing list a vital part of our lives. Thanks so much for your support and encouragement.

One of the major problem areas that needs some understanding and discussion is masturbation. It is a delicate subject, to say the least. I want to make it clear that this subject is being discussed only within the context of the Christian who is attempting to lead a celibate life. This is not an attempt to deal with this controversial problem in a broad sense, but only as it directly effects *us*. First of all, it is most important to state that research clearly shows that masturbation is not strictly a homosexual problem. This practice, particularly in younger people, does not in itself point to homosexual tendencies, but is a widespread problem of all sexual identities and ages. It is necessary for us to realize that the practice or involvement in it, to whatever degree, does not point the finger of guilt at gay people exclusively.

I know only too well how masturbation can be a problem with people who are being denied sexual contacts because of their Christian commitment. It is more of a problem with some than with others. God seems to be dealing with people at different levels in various ways. It often becomes a trap, and we keep falling into it. The greatest harm is the guilt and condemnation that it produces. Then there are the fantasies to contend with and what they do to your mental outlook. The fantasies are always present, and this is the greatest danger. The act itself probably is of no great consequence, but it is never the act alone, and thus the problem compounds itself. I'm not saying the act is right. I'm only saying that it is rarely isolated and can turn into a pattern that can cripple a person's Christian walk. There are many opinions about this subject and whether it is right or wrong. The majority of our group feels that it is something that every Christian, gay or straight, should attempt to grow away from. Mainly, it is an act that tends to quench the Holy Spirit. God certainly forgives us of all our confessed sins, past, present, and future, but that is not a license to continue doing something that might hurt our relationship with Him. It is really a matter of attitude. We want to grow in the Lord and we want to walk in His Spirit. Part of this is an attempt to guard our thought-lives. Any of us can stumble and fall, or make mistakes, but then we need to give these things to God to deal with. It is impossible to remain in the Spirit and practice any act that will shut Him out. The idea is to grow in the right direction and attempt to resolve some of these problem areas. Pray and be strict with yourself, but above all, if you stumble, don't get into the guilt and condemnation trip. Just point yourself back in the right direction and keep trying. With some it might be a long and difficult battle, but we have a loving and understanding God, and He knows what we are going through.

Regarding pitfalls, I would like to say that we have a good tape on this subject by Brother Frank. If you are interested, we would be happy to send it to you for two dollars. Each one of us has different views as to what constitutes a pitfall. We have all experienced different ones, and if we are to successfully pursue the Christian walk and conquer life's problems, then we have to avoid them. Masturbation can be one, as we have already discussed. It is something that can evolve into a deadly situation and can lead us to fall. Another is going to gay bars or gay parties and mixing with former friends that have no interest in the Christian life. We are just asking for trouble by doing this, even under the guise of "witnessing." It can be a dangerous pitfall. I could go on listing many "don'ts" in our daily dealing with life, but I would not be giving you any credit for the God-given conviction within your own heart. Let's be honest. If we're serious about what we are doing, and our commitment means something, then we have to step ahead into a new life style that is Christlike. That means cleaning up our lives. It means steering clear of all the old habit patterns that held us firm in the gay life. Changing relationships, avoiding old temptations, dropping mannerisms—whatever—this is our new direction. Satan is right there pulling every dirty trick in the book to make you fall, and we must all consciously avoid pitfalls that will drag us down. We must boldly turn from situations that could pull us down. We all know our own weaknesses. It is God's will that we turn from them and walk with Him instead.

I would like to end by reviewing the book *Sons of Freedom: God and the Single Man*, by Gini Andrews (Zondervan). This was a most interesting book, although directed primarily to younger heterosexuals.

Even so, there is much to be learned from this fresh and challenging point of view. Although much of the book does not apply to us, it does have an excellent chapter entitled "Forever Gay?" Basically, Miss Andrews restates what we already hold, that homosexuality is wrong in God's eyes, and that He never intended this type of relationship among men and women. I believe that she has presented her feelings and thoughts with love and compassion, and feel that her concern and outreach are genuine. It is important that you read literature on this subject. What makes Miss Andrews' point of view so important is that she takes a firm stand on what she believes, and speaks out on the strength of her faith in Jesus Christ and what He can do for us. She states without any doubt whatever that, providing we have the willingness to change, in time God *will* heal and change us and make us new. To quote her reference, Galatians 4:7, 5:1 promises that "We are no longer slaves, but God's own sons. . . . Christ has made us free." She asks, "Should we have added 'This does not apply to homosexuals, and abandon hope all ye who are in this class?' Hardly! This great promise is for us all, and nothing is impossible for God." Praise Him for people like Gini Andrews who hold firm in the power of the blood of Christ, of the resurrected Lord and the Holy Spirit.

Have courage. You are in our prayers always,

Bob

* * *

Dear Friends,   March, 1976

It is exciting and encouraging to receive so many wonderful letters from all over the United States and to know that we are in your prayers. It builds great strength in us to realize that so many are behind us in our ministry and that our outreach extends to far distant places. You are all very close to our hearts and you are in our daily prayers. We want to share our victories as well as our burdens, that we might build one another up in the body of Christ and minister to your needs and concerns. I have tried to answer every letter personally, but things are getting ahead of me now, and others in our fellowship will be sharing in the correspondence to those of you who have written. It is an opportunity to get to know others in our group, which continues to grow each month. We praise our Lord for bringing in such wonderful people, not only here in San Rafael but all over America, as an extension of this outreach to Christians with homosexual backgrounds. Our prayer is that some of you might begin groups such as ours to minister directly to those in need around your community. We can help you by announcing news of such beginnings here in the newsletter, and refer people to an address or a post office box. If you are starting a group or intend to, and want this publicized, let us know.

We have added three new people to our regular fellowship this past month and I want to share with you the joy that these people bring to us. We want to encourage and build them up, but they in turn build us up as well and give us great strength. God knows our hearts and can see the commitment here, as well as the sacrifice, and I know He will mold His children into new creatures that are dedicated to His service. It takes a special kind of commitment to Jesus Christ to be willing to carry the burdens that are involved, much more than the average Christian needs to give. A heterosexual must make changes also, to be sure, but his new birth does not require him to enter a world totally foreign, nor does it require total celibacy, perhaps for life. It is not a matter of giving up "bad habits." It is a matter of changing your entire nature, as you know and live it, moving from the familiar and secure to the unfamiliar and insecure. To you that minister to us, it would be the same as being asked to reverse your complete sexual orientation, and after doing it, remaining celibate as well. I doubt if you could do it, but we are expected to do it easily, as though we were being asked to give up smoking or lying or swearing. I can assure you that this is no exaggeration. We must ask you counselors to say it with love, and be patient, and have the understanding of Christ himself. Don't judge us if we have problems. We love Jesus and we need time to grow.

This month I would like to focus in on two other main issues that are of great concern to our people. The first is the problem of leading a double life. Gays in general are coming out of the "closet" in great numbers these days. The changes in this direction in recent years are earthshaking. Many homosexuals, particularly young ones, are choosing to be totally open about their sexual orientation. This seems to be the direction in which the gay community is moving. Hardly a day goes by without an article about gay rights in the news media. However, many gays still lead distinctly double lives. Usually, their private world is different and apart from their public world. Some are totally "in the closet" and mask their homosexuality completely, living a fairly "straight" life, and keeping their sexual preferences secret. There are many variations as well as exceptions. The point is made only in reference to the challenge of those of us who have elected to change because of our Christianity. Here the double life continues to exist in most cases. Many of us still choose to hide our homosexuality in order to function in the straight world and avoid hurt and ridicule. Others have chosen to witness to their change, both to straights as well as unsaved gays, and have had to face ridicule even from supposedly "loving Christians." Frightening! The Holy Spirit has a big job to do in the hearts of believers. The fact remains that there are few alternatives. In our position, there are really only two choices, and I have already stated them. You either openly admit what you are (or were) and attempt to fit into the Christian community, or you try to "go it straight" for all outward purposes, so that as God heals and builds you up, He can make you into that new person. I suppose there is a kind of "in-between." One would simply be the person they feel they are and go on growing in Christ with the expectation that He will continue to strengthen and bring one into the fullness of His glory. Each one of us must do what we are led to do in our heart. Above all, though, we need to release our lives to Him, and then He can bring us into new life in His perfect way.

The second and final concern I want to bring to you this month is that of the self-imposed sadness that we often bring on ourselves as a means of comforting ourselves. Kent spoke on this subject a couple of months ago in our group devotions. It is called melancholy. People with any kind of emotional problem often fall victim to this. I have used it myself in earlier days, and we bring it on ourselves as a defense. We attempt to cope with our situations by bringing on this self-pity and "poor me" set of feelings. It seems to ease the pain for the moment, but in the end it only leads to depression. It is so easy and comfortable to fall into this pattern. You get lonely and begin to feel sorry for yourself. You think about all you are missing, and how life has been so cruel. And it has, without a doubt. But you are a new creature, no matter what your circumstance. I am a strong believer in Romans 8:28 and know that God will use every situation for good for those that love Him and are called according to His purpose. Some of you might say "But you're not in *my* position. How can you say that?" It's true, I'm not, but our God is big, and nothing is impossible for Him, no matter where you are or what you're up against. Jesus does not enter into sadness, but has a true sense of compassion. Philippians 4:8 is such a contrast to melancholy. He commands us not to dwell on sadness and loneliness but to rejoice and dwell on all the beautiful things in our walk with Him. Satan would have us wallow in self-pity and remorse, but Christ would have us free, emptying ourselves as He emptied himself (Phil. 2:5-7). Read Hebrews 4:14-16. It means so much to me. I pray that it will touch your heart as well. Have courage.

Love in Christ,
Bob

* * *

Easter Greetings to You All   April 1976
  This is a special season for us and an exciting time to

158

reflect upon our Lord Jesus Christ and what He accomplished at Calvary for each of us. As I think about the events of this past week and their celebration throughout the Christian church, it is especially significant to relate them in light of the struggles that each of us face. Our day-to-day walk with the Lord is strengthened greatly when we are able to focus upon what Jesus did two thousand years ago. His carrying the burden in our behalf, His taking our sin upon himself to end it once and for all, His total and complete forgiveness, because He loved us more than we can comprehend, and died to save us. We think about these things frequently, but we bring them to mind in a new and fresh way each Easter season. It becomes a time of renewal as we look ahead to further growth throughout the coming year. We realize afresh that the abounding love shown in that act continues today as He lifts us up and makes us free. Praise the Lord! He lives!

We continue to receive many exciting and rewarding letters. Some of you have shared many beautiful things in your lives. You have also shared difficult times, doubts, sorrows, sadness and heavy burdens. One of the most supportive things we can do is to keep you all in our prayers. We also attempt to write personally to each of you in response to your letters, but please be patient. This has been a busy time, and as mentioned last month, we are trying to spread out the correspondence in order for you to meet others in our ministry.

We want to share with you our excitement over the cooperation we have received from Peninsula Bible Church in Palo Alto. Their love and concern for Christians with homosexual backgrounds is so evident from the letters we have received in answer to the newsletter. I had written to Pastor Ray Stedman last year after hearing him speak on the subject of homosexuality at Mount Hermon, California during the summer of 1975. I sent him the book *The Third Sex?* and thanked him for his interest and informed him of our outreach here. Since that time we have heard from PBC regularly and are thankful for their growing outreach to the gay community. It is thrilling for us to be able to share with this fine church and we are thankful for their love. I just praise God for this vital aspect of His perfect work.

Last month I spoke at length about living "the double life." The position taken reflected the thinking of our group here, but certainly does not include all aspects of the problems faced by each us us. I would like to say a few more things about this subject. At the risk of repeating myself, it is necessary to reaffirm the idea that each person must make his or her own choices. We must exercise our own will, as God would have us do in all things, and it must be right for us. What you feel today may not reflect what you felt a year ago, or be consistent with what you may feel in the future. It is *now* that counts, and then we continue to grow and are molded in accordance with what God is able to do in our lives and as we are open to *His* will. Christians with deep and harsh gay backgrounds are going to find the road rougher perhaps than someone new to gay life. God has more work to do in some us than in others, but above all we must be open to whatever changes He wants to make in us. We so often say that we can't change, that it's impossible. Sometimes it seems that way, but nothing is impossible for God, only as we see ourselves, but certainly not as *He* sees us. What is my point? For some it will continue to be a double life of sorts. As we step out into a new and changed life, the old hangs on like a dark cloud. We may choose to hide what we were, pushing it back from our memory as much as possible. Then again, some feel that to be really free, we must openly admit it, not blatantly, but as we are led, a testimony to our commitment and to what God is doing in our lives. Free at last, no more lies, holding our heads high with dignity. But perhaps you're not ready for that yet. Perhaps you'll never be. Free means to be what is right for you, to make the choice that God leads you to make. We give it to Him to deal with, knowing that He will accomplish it all. As for me, I want to be the new person that God has promised, free to be a completely changed man, to use the trials and struggles as strengthening agents to bear the burdens and to help others through the darkness. My new life is committed to Him.

The other day we received a letter asking if we were a commune, all living together as one unit of people. It made me realize that we take for granted that others know fully where we are. Our local group here in San Rafael is made up of about ten to twelve Christians from the greater San Francisco Bay Area. We all come from different church affiliations, and meet regularly together on alternate Thursday evenings to share together, minister to each other, have devotions and pray. Our spiritual adviser is Rev. Kent Philpott of Church of the Open Door in San Rafael who first started this outreach to gays and wrote the book *The Third Sex?* based on the lives of six of us. We come from

161

all walks of life and all different experiences, but our common bonds are our new lives in Christ and our homosexual backgrounds. All people within geographic reach of San Rafael are free to join with us in a common commitment to Jesus Christ. We are not a closed organization, except for the restriction that those interested must have been involved in the gay life at some time or have homosexual tendencies.

Coming next month: in the May issue will be a guest newsletter from Kent. We know that you will be blessed by his message to you. In the June issue will be a review of the recent article in *Christianity Today* entitled "Open Door to Gays: Grounds For Separation."

The following list of tapes is being offered to you this month and are available for purchase at three dollars each, which includes postage and handling. They are all recordings of sermons preached by Kent. These tapes are *not* oriented to homosexuals specifically, but are of general interest to Christians as a body. The titles are: Theology of Praise, The Three in One, Sex and the Bible, Biblical Demonology, Some Things You Should Know About God, The Normal Christian Family, The Gospel According to Peter, On Women, The Church: The Body of Christ, and Some Facts About the Second Coming. If you are interested in any of these, send orders to Christian General Store, 2130 Fourth Street, San Rafael, California 94901. Make checks payable to the same.

May this Easter season be a special blessing to all of you as you continue to grow in our Lord Jesus Christ.

In His Name,
Bob

* * *

Greetings dear brothers and sisters,   May 1976

For this month of May, our fellowship group has asked me to write the newsletter, and I am happy for the opportunity. It seems I have a mountain of emotion and love I want to share with you, and at the same time I know this simple letter will not allow me to be to you all that I want. So please read between the lines.

This ministry God has given us has expanded beyond what we anticipated. And with the growth comes additional pressure and responsibility. We find that we will be needing a full-time counselor (perhaps more), an office, and we want to be able to have a conference in August dealing with the church and ministry to the homosexual who wants to follow Jesus and move out of the gay life. A sizable ministry of correspondence and tapes has grown up too and we will need to meet this more effectively. We have no desire to build an empire in any way. Years ago I helped develop a system of Christian houses over parts of the country and it eventually became a monster that devoured itself. Rather than getting into big Christian business and enterprises, we want to help others develop ministries such as Love in Action, upon request. Our purpose is to see God develop stable work here that others can learn from and carry workable principles into their own areas. This has been working to a small degree already. When we first began these newsletters I emphasized to Bob that we would never make an appeal for funds. Now we face a situation where we need to operate with greater freedom but are handicapped because we don't have the money. Our needs are not gigantic but very real. We feel we need an office where we can freely counsel, meet, work out of, etc. Also we need to be able to give someone a minimal salary to administer the growing work load. And last of all, our conference for late summer will cost us some money. We bring in some funds ourselves but not enough to do the job. Personally, my church provides for my financial needs. I don't need any money at all. This is not a full-time ministry with me, either. Our board of pastors has given me a free hand to develop the work as I can so there is no financial pressure on me. So we are opening the door to any who feel led of God to do it, to become personally involved with us through your offerings. As I write this I feel apologetic for having to say this, and I know the others will too, but with confidence I must share with you these things. There would be no need to speak of this had it not been for the growth of Love in Action. We do have a non-profit tax deductible corporation called House Ministries that was incorporated in September 1973. This ministry forms the legal covering for Love in Action. We can issue receipts then. A check must be made out to House Ministries with Love in Action written at the bottom. There is no administrative charge so all the money that comes in is for Love In Action exclusively.

I've just finished Judson Cornwall's book on praise called *Let Us Praise* (Logos). In over two hundred times in the Bible we are called on, even commanded, to praise. The Scripture is filled with passages on praise. Some great ones are: Psalm 9:1-2, 33:1-3, Psalm 100 and 150, Matthew 21:14-17, Acts 3:8, Hebrews 13:15, and Ephesians 1:12. Let me quote these last two. "Through him [Jesus] then let us continually offer up a sacrifice of praise to God, that is, the fruit of lips that acknowledge his name," and "We who first hoped in Christ have been destined and appointed to live for the praise of his glory." It's easy to see that praise is very central to the Christian life. But why then don't we praise much? Let me offer a few ideas. One, the fear of man. Remember the hard-hitting statement, "They loved the praise of men more than the praise of God." C.S. Lewis, in a very wonderful little work entitled *Reflections on the Psalms,* said that fear and shyness hindered praise. That is true of most of us, but we need to put it behind us and will with the security that Jesus gives us. Two, our self-centeredness. It is very hard to praise God when we are so into ourselves. We are often tied up and crammed into tiny boxes. Praise gives us a wonderful release and increases our delight and completes us. Three, often people who do not praise have not grasped the reality of Christ, nor have they claimed the power of His blood to forgive sin. When we see the greatness of what He has done for us in comparison to our total lostness, it should cause us to praise. Four, ignorance, that is, some people simply do not know that they are commanded to praise. Praise is not a philpottism, a cornwallism, or any kind of-ism. It is just Bible and normal Christianity. Five, we have falsely equated emotionalism with praise, with the accompanying error that emotionalism is bad. Let me ask, "Is all emotionalism bad?" "No" many would say, "just when it comes to God and religion." You know, that is just not true. How can you do something sincerely and not be emotionally involved? You can't, and this is certainly true when love is involved. Where there is love, there will be emotionalism. We are too fearful of

Elmer Gantry or Marjoe. Emotionalism for the pure sake of emotionalism certainly is not balanced or healthy, but praise to God is healthy. C.S. Lewis said, "Praise almost seems to be inner health made audible" (from *Reflections on the Psalms*). Six, the attitude, "That's not my style" deludes many. What do we care about style? If it was good enough for King David, it is good enough for me. Right? People who don't know anything about football can blandly sit through even the most exciting game. But the person who knows what's going on down on the field is bound to get excited. It is not a question of style, it is a question of knowing what God is doing and who God is. When you know that, you will praise. Seven, Satan wants to squelch praise. If you are in a state of mind where you have an enemy, you definitely don't want to have that enemy praised by anyone. Now consider how Satan hates to have people praise his enemy.

It is only fair at this point for me to offer some points on how to praise God. One, it is an act of our will. We must *decide* to praise Him. Two, we can obey His command to praise Him. The Word says, "Praise ye the Lord" many times. Three, begin to praise Him with your whole life, words, and works. You can't do one without the other. Four, praise God for who He is and not on the basis of how you feel. Five, open your heart to be filled with God's Spirit that He might help you to praise. Six, learn to praise. Martin Luther said, "To praise the Lord with gladness is not a work of man. It cannot be taught in words, but must be learned in one's experience." This is not the last word on praise, but it may be a help and encouragement to someone.

Thank you for letting me share this with you. I thank

God that we are all involved in this work together. To God be the glory, forever and ever, Amen.

Kent Philpott

*   *   *

Dear Friends,   June 1976

Summer is almost upon us and it is a great feeling to see the beauty everywhere and be refreshed by the warm sunshine. When I look out at the hills and trees, I marvel at God's perfect design and praise Him for the majesty all around.

Last month we received a beautiful tape letter from Roberta, author of *Gay Liberation*, who lives in Michigan. It was a blessing. She is a dear sister who has ministered to all of us, and several of our people here in San Rafael originally met us through her excellent ministry. We consider her a very important part of our outreach and ask that all of you lift her up in prayer. If any of you would care to write her personally, she would be delighted to hear from you. Her address is: Roberta, 4191 44th St., S. E., Grand Rapids, Michigan, 49508. We have great hopes of her coming out to San Rafael some time this year, and we have been holding that request up to God. Her tape has been circulating among our people here, and many of them will be dropping her a note. We have hopes that she will make a tape especially designed to be added to our tape ministry. We praise the Lord for her witness.

Two months ago I mentioned that I would review the article in *Christiantiy Today* entitled "Open Doors to Gays: Grounds For Separation?" Basically this article is nothing more than an update on the controversial action taken in Santa Clara County (California) by their Council of Churches in admitting the Metropolitan Community Church of San Jose (a gay church) to membership, and the subsequent furor it created. At the writing of the article, five member churches had withdrawn from the council as a result of this action, and more were contemplating withdrawal. The article goes on to discuss the various attitudes towards MCC and whether it is an action that has scriptural basis. All of the standard arguments are cited, and no real conclusions are drawn. And so it goes, back and forth between the two factions. The council has stated that the admittance of MCC was not intended to condone homosexuality, but that an outreach to a little-understood group of people is needed within the Christian community. One of the basic issues, however, is stated to be the authority of the Scriptures. One opinion voiced by the minority side of the council stated that the action was in effect "institutionalizing sin." It was also cited that several medical and sociological assertions pointed to homosexuality as a learned behavior. Since this behavior is rejected by the Bible they reason it can be *un*learned and cleansed through Christ. In any case, the majority won out, and MCC churches all over the United States are gradually being admitted to various councils on that basis. Love in Action has stated openly in previous publications that we do not support the doctrinal view of MCC toward homosexuality, but there is no question about the fact that Christ's church, as His body, does need to reach out to the gay community in love and acceptance, but within the framework of a desire to become the persons God intended us to be. What God wants is exactly what we are seeking.

As we reach out to people in our ministry here, the one topic that continues to repeat itself without apparent solution is that of dealing with sexual drives. That surely is the understatement of the times. It is the root of a multitude of problems and anxieties. Most of our counseling deals with the impact of human sexuality. This, of course, is true of the heterosexual world as well. Current news would attest to that fact. Sexual drives in homosexuals are very strong, way above average, I think we would all agree. They gay life style revolves around sexuality and all its counterparts. So, moving from that arena of activity to that of the Christian life style and following the teachings of the Bible is a large order. Even with the determined attempt to make a new life in Jesus and focus our attention on Him, the "old nature" still hangs on. This is true of every Christian who is dealing with the former self. But, as is true of any person that was involved in "heavy" sin—alcohol, drugs, incest, whatever—the depth of what went on before leaves an indelible scar on the emotions, and the memories never seem to fade. The mind becomes an instant-replay catalog of events and experiences that are forever coming into mental view the moment we relax the mind, or see a visual reminder of our past, of which there seems to be an endless flow. How to deal with this very real problem is a crucial part of our ministry and there is no easy, quick method of solution. Looking to God is, of course, "the answer." I really believe that. But at the same time I recognize that God is not choosing to "zap" any of us with instant healing, and at the same time, erase all the memories that continue to plague each of us. Thus, we seem to fend for ourselves, trying desperately to do it, and failing over and over. But wait. I thought God was the answer! And He is! So why not let Him do it? Sounds so trite, doesn't it, and yet it's true and it's real. The problem is, we want to be "zapped." We don't want to wait because the struggles are too rough. It is heavy to the point of becoming almost impossible.

This very weekend one of our brothers said to me, "How can I last through even one more year of this?" I said in response, "How can I last one more week?" But I will last, and so will he. We have each other, and the sharing and fellowship and caring are God's ingredients to healing, long-lasting healing that will impart strength as God does it in *His* time and not in *ours*. So we continue to hold together, supporting one another in every way possible, bearing the hardships as Christ himself bore them. We stumble along, making mistake after mistake, but He forgives and forgets, and we pick ourselves up and start back up the mountain. I am reminded of the very first Christian book I ever read when I first became a renewed Christian. It was written by Hannah R. Hurnard and is entitled *Hinds' Feet on High Places*. It is what is called an allegory in literature, and is about the strangest book I have ever read in my life. This book really spoke to me and is a true picture of a Christian's struggles in the attempt to walk through life with Jesus in an effort to reach the highest peak of "perfection." A hind is a very sure-footed mountain animal, able to walk on the most rugged of high, rocky places without falling, and we would all like to have hinds' feet in our climb up the rocky road of life. The beauty of the whole story, which is God's precious promise, is that we will reach it. And He is at our side even now as we go stumbling along. Praise the Lord!

May all of you develop the greatest strength in your effort to reach the "high places."

Yours in Jesus,
Bob

* * *

Dear Friends   July 1976

Last month I was looking out at God's perfect design and praising Him for the beauty all around, and I still am, but it grieves me so to see the parched land of California, stricken with the worst drought I have ever experienced in my life. The weather conditions here, and in many places all over the world, give ominous feelings and a certain mystery of how God deals with His land. No rain, and we are experiencing extremes that are frightening. All season, thus far, the winds have blown relentlessly across the dry, brown landscape.

In late June our friends at Peninsula Bible Church in Palo Alto sent us a copy of a book I had never seen before, *The Returns of Love* by Alex Davidson (Inter-Varsity). Its subtitle is "Letters of a Christian Homosexual," and I can tell you that it was one of the most beautiful books that I have read on this subject. I think it is "must" reading for all of us and deals with many problem areas that are of great concern to us. I was deeply touched by it, and it has led me to share with you this month some new insights that God has given me on the subject of love. After all, our goal is to put love in real action, a love that is so deep and so fulfilling that it gives us an enabling power to do the impossible. So much has been written on this subject. We get tired of hearing about it, quite often, because it is confusing and vague. The Bible has much to say about love and "God *is* love," and Christians without love can do nothing.

I have to give a word of personal testimony here in order to set the stage for this new awareness. When I was in the gay life style, I had plenty of love to give and I gave it to those I chose and very few others. It was the only love I knew and it was a very fragile sort that I never understood. The feelings ran very deep quite often, but in many cases were extremely shallow and short-lived. I was a very selfish person and gave of myself only to the degree that was comfortable and pleasurable. It was a fully self-centered kind of giving. After I became a new Christian and chose to be a new person in Christ, I struggled desperately to understand this other level of love that I was supposed to cultivate. I failed repeatedly (and still do), and became miserable because it kept relating to the old kind that was so familiar and comfortable. I asked God over and over to help me know this kind of love, but it never became clear. Gradually, I did begin to learn to care more about others and to feel this new kind of love that I realized must be "it." It felt good, but it still didn't fulfull nor enable me to do anything in a very powerful way. What was wrong? I finally began to realize that it was because I was still more interested in myself. My focus was still on me and my image as it had always been. But it was so hard to break away, to start getting my eyes on others and away from myself.

But in becoming the new person in Christ, I discovered that I was stepping out of one closet into another. I was sort of a "non-person," turning from the old self with *its* level of love into someone that could only express agape love at a distance. It became clear. God had led me to a place where I knew I could not remain. I had to walk through that door, out into the whole world, to be *in* it but not *of* it, and to reach out to others as He reached out. No, I can't do it, Lord. Please, can't I just hide? Can't I be my new self in some quiet corner and love people from a distance? I was smothering. I had to do it, and God wanted *me* to make the choice. I fought and twisted, and it hurt, but it was no use. I had to go through that door, and I did. This has been just in the past year, since last summer. I stepped out in a new way to all my brothers and sisters, gay and straight, and began loving them and caring about them in a way that was totally new. This brings us back full circle to Mr. Davidson's book, because I was experiencing the returns of love one hundredfold. I was finally able to take my eyes off myself and keep them on others in a new way. I began to realize that when you can love people so deeply and so sincerely that it creates a bond between you, that suddenly the fullness comes, and with it the enabling power of Jesus Christ in your life to tackle anything. Then the real healing comes, and it's beautiful.

But if we reach that point, why do we keep failing? Is there never an end to the unremitting struggles? asks Alex Davidson. And the New Testament replies with the great doctinre of the resurrection of the body. Romans 8:10-11 is one of the important passages. When Christ bestows eternal life and enters a man's heart, it is a new *spiritual* life. The old physical body is still dead to sin, but the promise is there, for eventually we will have new bodies as well, all the old faults and infirmities that caused us so much trouble will be gone, and we will be raised and re-created in perfection for the world to come. Mr. Davidson points out, "The fact that the Spirit already dwells in me, so that in spite of frequent failure I truly do delight in the law of God after the inward man, is the guarantee that one day the renewal of the body will follow." So in our newness of spirit, let us step out and heed the message that "ye have heard from the beginning, that we should love one another," in a committing way that will bind us together in Christ Jesus now and forever.

God has placed in my heart the message that I have brought to you this month. But it is not just my message, but one that we here in San Rafael have talked over many times. It has brought us closer together as a result. Beyond our own thoughts, however, is God's own message of Colossians 3:12-15. "As God's chosen . . . clothe yourselves with tenderness of heart, kindliness, humility, gentleness, patient endurance. Bear with one another and forgive each other in case one has a grievance against another. Just as the Lord has forgiven you, so do you. *But crown it all with love, which is the perfect bond of union.* And let the peace of Christ, to which you were called in one body, arbitrate in your hearts. And be thankful" (New Berkeley Version, italics mind).

May the Lord bless your lives to the degree that will allow love to flow in an abundance that you never knew possible.

Yours in Jesus,
Bob

* * *

Dear Friends,   August 1976

During this past year we have talked about many issues and concerns that are on the hearts of most Christians with homosexual backgrounds. We have tried to grasp some insights into the reality of life as we live it, and attempt to focus in on what God has for us in terms of tomorrow. It is never easy, for tomorrow remains a mystery, a guessing game that centers around the uncertainties of our defeats and our victories. No matter how we view these problems, it is only one perspective of a whole array of thoughts and ideas that flow from people whose lives are connected in some measure to God and His design for each of us. Some problems come up over and over again, and often a second or third look is needed into a particular area as God continues to work in our lives in an effort to smooth the rough places. We certainly don't claim to have the answers, but our Lord has led us to share the thoughts on our hearts that we might impart to each of you a closer understanding of what it means to walk this narrow road.

One of the issues that frequently comes up is the sin nature of homosexuality. There is much written on this subject, and a great deal preached about it, some of it in error. Kent Philpott has written about this topic in his book, and various other books have touched on it to one degree or another. There was an excellent chapter on the subject in *The Returns of Love*. Our position is unchanged and has been discussed generally in previous newsletters. Homosexuality *is* a sin, and God's Word clearly shows us this valuable truth. But that statement is not enough. Further clarification is needed since such a statement is too broad and general. We need to be more specific because people aren't really clear about what that message says. We need to consider the difference between the *condition* of homosexuality and that of the *practice* of homosexuality. Scripture condemns the open practice of homosexuality with all its acts, the actual overt involvement in the gay life. Messages on this idea are often unclear as to exactly what is being referred to in condemning gays. Some ministers are guilty of pronouncing judgment on homosexuals in general, without defining specifically what they mean. What is often meant is total condemnation, and if a person has any degree of these tendencies, Christian or not, he or she is unable to come under God's grace and forgiveness. How gross! What a perversion of God's Word. What a twisting of the beautiful meanings of justification and sanctification. The Christian church can hang its head in utter shame at the shabby way it has treated gay people over the generations. Fear and prejudice run rampant whenever the subject comes up.

But let's continue our point. While the practice of homosexual acts is labeled sin, the condition is most definitely not. Let's be careful here. Do not misunderstand. All I am saying is that any man or woman who discovers homosexual tendencies, at whatever point in life that might be, or to whatever degree of intensity they might be, that condition in itself is not sin. Sin enters the picture when the overt act becomes a reality, along with the accompanying life style. This partially explains why Christians who have turned from the gay life to follow Jesus Christ still might have the condition in varying degrees. The condition has to be separated from the action or involvement in the scene as a whole. As Christians we know that our confessed sin (all of it) is forgiven and forgotten. But some of us still feel condemned because we still have the condition. Spiritual warfare rages on because we are supposedly new creatures in Christ, the old has passed away. But it is still there. Why? Our old nature is dead to sin, but it hangs on like a weight around us and will until we die. We may move far away from it in our spiritual climb with Christ, but some of us may indeed have that "thorn in the flesh" day in and day out. We are talking about the old carnal nature here, not about a particular sin. The old has passed away, but will not be separated from us until we rid ourselves of this sin-nature body, and be with *Him* face to face. What a precious promise! So there's quite a difference in "being homosexual" with all its psychological and emotional strains and stresses, and actively choosing to participate in a life of sin that God clearly labels wrong. Remember we are new spiritual beings, righteous in God's sight, wholly new and clean. Stop condemning yourself (if you still are) and remember that you are one of God's precious children, filled with His Holy Spirit, that will empower you to deal with the old person. Praise the Lord for new life, even when the old nags at us. God tells us that out of our weakness comes His strength.

Where then do we go from here? What is the next step after that concept has been grasped? How do we step into the fullness of life that God intends instead of retreating into a sexual third world? The answer to that question is as broad as the complexity of human nature itself. Each and every case will be somewhat different depending on environment, circumstances, experience, age, and, above all, attitude. One's image of himself bears greatly on growth as well. Progress can be exceedingly slow or even quite fast, depending on the combination of these and other factors. But, one thing we can say without question. Regardless of any of these conditions, nothing will ever happen in newness of life until *you*, the individual, take that necessary step of faith, that act of self-determination, to move forward into the life that Christ has made available to you. He wants *us* to make some choices. Too many Christians step back and ask God to do all the work, to give all the gifts, to do all the healing. We have to wake up to the fact that God, through His Holy Spirit dwelling within us, wants each individual to step forward and act upon the strengths and victories that are already his or hers. Then true and complete healing *is* possible because you have opened wide the door for God to work miracles in your life. When we get to the point that we believe that Christ provided it all, and step out and claim it, then we can begin to be the new creatures that we already are in His eyes.

May God give you a vision for tomorrow, that you might lay hold of the truths that already exist.

Love in Christ,
Bob

* * *

Greetings to you all,   September 1976

In past newsletters we have made several references to the Peninsula Bible Church in Palo Alto, California, and the help and cooperation we have received from them. This dynamic church is doing much in reaching out to many segments of society to bring the good news of Jesus Christ, and we are thankful for their fine ministry and help to us. All the messages given to that congregation are reproduced in printed form as an extension of their ministry, and these printed messages have been made available all over the world through Discovery Publishing, the publications ministry of PBC. During the course of the last year, three of these excellent messages have come to our attention as being particularly significant in speaking to the Christian with homosexuality in his or her background. They are not addressed specifically to gays, or ex-gays, but the very nature of the content we think will bless each of you greatly. This month, through the cooperation and generosity of PBC, we are making the first of these messages available to you as an enclosure to our newsletter. (The remaining two will be coming in later issues.) It is an Easter sermon delivered at that church by the famed author and speaker Mr. Hal Lindsey on April 18, 1976. We are convinced that it will bless you as much as it did us.

Next month we hope to bring to you a report on the EXIT Seminar in Anaheim held by Melodyland Christian Center during the weekend of September 10-12. We are very excited about what God is doing in the ministry to homosexuals, and we are convinced that He is giving us some new insights into the problems of reaching our fellow brothers and sisters. So be looking for that report in the October issue. Also, we will be bringing you an updated listing of the tapes that we have available. Some of our tapes have been redone and new ones added. The long awaited "Brother Bob" tape that I had hopes of completing early this year is finally finished and now available. For those of you who have read *The Third Sex?*, this tape picks up on my life from where the book leaves off and describes some of the things that have taken place over this past year or so. It also gives you some of my ideas and thoughts on the "new life in Christ" and some words of encouragement.

There have been instances in past newsletters when I have discussed issues or questions more than one time, and attempted to explain that further investigation was often necessary into some of the "heavier" problems that we deal with. One of these issues is that of the "gay identity." I want to make clear what I mean by this term and put it into the context of our ministry. I am speaking about the issue of the Christian with a homosexual background dealing with the whole problem of identity as being "gay" or "ex-gay." This is an extremely delicate area and very controversial. There are as many opinions and theories prevailing as one would find on any controversial issue. There are no "pat" answers, and only God himself knows the real truth. But I think it helps to discuss it in light of what is going on in all of our lives. Let us understand that we are talking about men and women who have turned from the gay life style with all of its involvement, and have now chosen to follow the teachings of Jesus Christ. I am not referring to Christians who have chosen to continue to live the gay life style and pursue sexual and love relations within that framework. The identity issue is clear in those cases.

Christians who have chosen to step out into new life and have made the step toward turning from the old nature are faced with the problem of their continued "gayness." There are many degrees of gay identification evident in the lives of all of us in this position. They range from "totally identifying as always being homosexual, regardless of one's walk with Christ" to the opposite extreme of being "ex-gay . . . no longer a homosexual . . . the old life dead, gone, finished and over . . . in effect, a heterosexual." Then there are all the degrees in between. I have spoken about this issue in my new tape, and our enclosure this month gives many insights into this line of thinking—the old versus the new. *Our* thinking is based mainly on what God says to us in the Bible about our new life in Christ. If we are truly a "born-again" Christian and it is in fact a *real* experience, then we are called to claim our new lives and step out and be the new creatures that we are declared to be. God sees us as new creatures, not new *homosexual* creatures, however. Our homosexuality, to whatever degree we lay claim to involvement, is part of our old nature, just as any part of our old life is now dead to sin. Of course most gays would state that homosexuality is different than any other condition, and thus cannot be dealt with or thought of in those terms. (The Metropolitan Community Church and the whole idea of "God made us this way" line of thinking is contrary to this position.) The fact remains, our earthly natures are to be separated from our new spiritual natures in Christ and to continue to claim identity to the old inhibits the growth of the new.

Now this brings up additional problems. The claim is made, "But I *am* a homosexual, really, even though I lay claim to my new life. The old *hasn't* passed away." Sorry. That's *man's* thinking, not God's. As far as *He* is concerned, the old has passed away, the new has come. It is a matter of focus. Are you choosing to focus on

181

your homosexual "plight" or are you focusing on your new life in Him? Oh, yes, I know all about the old hanging on, the constant reminder of what went on before. I am aware how much a part of your life your identity is, your image of yourself as you always have been and all the things you deal with. God sees us as *ex-gay*, but He also sees us as struggling and dealing with the old nature with its spiritual warfare. He sees us and loves us as human beings with all of our problems and hang-ups. Whether you see yourself as gay or ex-gay is your choice, as it is mine. But stop telling God how *He* should see you. Someday this old self will be dead, gone and separated from our new life in Him. We will have new and glorified bodies just like His. You won't be taking your homosexuality to heaven with you. That nature is *already* dead in His eyes. If the identity problem is one of your things, then may our Lord help you to take your eyes off yourself and all your problems and zero in on Him and what He has already promised. Have strength and be brave for Him!

Love in Christ,
Bob

* * *

Dear Friends,   October 1976
This month we are enclosing the second of three printed messages given to us by the Peninsula Bible Church in Palo Alto, California. It is a sermon delivered by Pastor Ray C. Stedman to his congregation on May 16, 1976, and has been made available to us through the generosity of Discovery Publishing of PBC. We think all three messages will bless you, and are particularly helpful to Christians

with homosexual backgrounds. We had a tremendous response from the Lindsey article enclosed last month and have been told that it ministered personally to many people. We want to thank PBC for their support and encouragement.

We are happy to report that the EXIT Conference and Seminar held at Melodyland Christian Center in Anaheim, California, on September 10, 11 and 12 was a great success and a blessing to all of us. Delegates from all over the United States and Canada gathered together at the Hotline Center there to discuss all the aspects of homosexuality. This was the first conference of this type, and was hosted by Jim Kasper and Mike Bussee, directors of EXIT, a Christian ministry to gays. The weekend consisted of workshops, an exchange of ideas, information, tapes and literature, liberally mixed with personal ministry and fellowship. One of the key speakers was Dr. Walter Martin, author of *Kingdom of the Cults*. A coalition of all the ministries was formed at the conclusion of the conference, under the name EXODUS. You will be hearing more of this group in future issues as information becomes available to us. A great many personal needs were expressed and one of the greatest blessings received was the flow of God's love among all participants. It brought a unity that has been greatly needed since the first outreach began. Bringing the good news of Jesus Christ to the gay world is an exciting prospect and purpose. Thanks to Greg Reid of EAGLE Ministry for his fine article and summary of the conference highlights and I would like to repeat his biblical quotation of Isaiah 59:19: "When the enemy shall come in like a flood the Spirit of the LORD shall lift up a standard against him" (KJV).

The following is an updated list of the tapes that Love in Action now has available. They are two dollars each and may be ordered by sending to Brother Frank, P.O. Box 2655, San Rafael, California 94902. Checks should be made payable to "House Ministries" with "Love in Action" written somewhere on the face of the check. The tapes are: Introduction to Love in Action, Brother Frank Testimony, Pitfalls, How to Counsel a Homosexual, Rally Tape, Brother Bob Testimony, Ministering to the Homosexual, and Examination of Gay Theology.

Quite a number of people on our mailing list are there as a direct result of reading the book *The Third Sex?* and many others are referrals from other ministries, churches, or individuals who have either read our materials or met people who have. We are most thankful for the way God has worked in this ministry to bring hope and love to our fellow brothers and sisters in Christ. Actually, a new book is now needed, and with God's providing, that will be possible next year. In the meantime, it is hoped that *The Third Sex?* can go into its second printing, as the distribution that a published book has can reach out to a wide scope of people, and we certainly would not want that to stop until such time as a new book becomes a reality. If the book blessed you or spoke to you personally, it would be helpful to write a short letter expressing your feelings about its value. You can write directly to the publisher, Logos International, 201 Church Street, Plainfield, New Jersey 07061, Attention: Dan Malachuk.

In the remaining portions of the newsletter this month I would like to write about a few frustrations. There comes a time every now and then when a person needs to get things out in the open and "let off steam." We all have these times when problems or concerns get so bottled up inside that we want to explode. Suddenly, nothing seems to work: soothing counsel, reading Scripture, prayer, and all the other means that Christians use in dealing with life. (But of course we know afterwards that nothing worked because our focus was on ourselves and not on Him.) We were indulging in self-pity, depression, and all the pits we fall into with Satan's help. But yet we do it. Sometimes things just simply get to be too much and off we go. I've been through such a period this past month and so I speak from personal experience. It is the kind of behavior that eventually leads to open rebellion and literally "going off the deep end." But then God brings you back, and you realize that He allowed you to struggle through it. In so doing, He has taught you some new lessons and reinforced some old ones. God uses every situation in our lives to strengthen us even though we may not see it. Praise God for such love, such understanding and such patience!

Sometimes I get tired of facing the same old problems in my own life. Some people have the mistaken idea that those of us who minister to the needs of others have no needs of our own. In the mind's eye, we are seen as being on some kind of spiritual upper-level. (Ministers are frequently seen in this light.) And it turns people off. People say, "How can I ever get where *he* is? Look how spiritual he is! He has all the problems licked. What hope is there for me with *my* messed up life?" Nothing could be further from the truth. Granted that some people have things more "together" in their spiritual lives than others. But all of us have to cope with many unseen problems in our lives and perhaps it is because we try to hide behind a mask of spirituality. This is why God calls us to "bear one another's burdens," to recognize that none of us is perfect. We are all reaching out together to a God who is wonderful enough and powerful enough to deal with each of us where we are. That is why the accompanying article hits home so strongly. It speaks to this issue—suffering. We all go through it, some more than others, but when we are able to take our eyes off of ourselves and free ourselves from looking at others as more "spiritual," and look at *Him*, then we can really begin to rejoice.

We are all going to suffer trials, but praise God for someone who can see us through it, and we come out a better person because of it. May God's unmatched love fill you to overflowing that you might rise to the highest peak of joy, despite the pain inside.

Yours in Him,
Bob

* * *

Greetings from San Rafael, November 1976

The third and final message in a series of three that we are sending with the newsletter is enclosed this month, given to us by Peninsula Bible Church of Palo Alto. We hope that it brings further inspiration and edification as you read of the precious truths of the Book of Romans. Thank you, Discovery Publishing and PBC.

This month I would like to continue my discussion of dealing with frustrations, because so much of the correspondence coming in speaks to this problem, and also because I continue to deal with this in my own life. We all do, at various levels of intensity. Frustrations come and go and many of them stay on and on. They become agonizing as you wait for something to happen. And when nothing happens, they intensify further and become more painful. In some instances they bring tears, and we cry out in desperation. How can we continue to suffer through this? When will it all end? How can I go on facing it? This brings to mind the enclosure of last month, "Rejoicing in Suffering." I have read and reread that article and I agree with it and it makes sense. I most certainly do rejoice that I am a Christian and have Jesus Christ as my Lord and Savior. He *is* my hope and yours, and I know that we are called to bear the suffering, as He bore it. Our agony and pain are temporary and short-lived in terms of our eternal life with God, and what a small price to pay for the joy and peace of an eternity of freedom. *That* is rejoicing in suffering, but we still deal with it on a day-to-day basis in the reality of life. Though we are renewed spiritually, we still deal with the flesh. Although we rejoice that we are free in Him, we continue to agonize over the problems and frustrations in our lives. They are real and they hurt. So what do we do?

There is a wide age range in our local ministry, and we need all ages from all walks and all experiences in order to do what God calls us to do and have an effective ministry. Each case is different, but I often think about what a rough road ahead the younger people have who are experiencing all of their youthful yearnings. But yet I know that they have been spared much of the pain, and I am thankful for that, but I know they have much to deal with. The older group has been through certain trials and that doesn't make them special in any way whatsoever, except perhaps in the area of counsel about certain matters. We are often thought to have less problems to face in moving from the gay life style because we *are* older, have been through all the problems before, are "ready" to call it quits, and are past our prime, so to speak. Well, that may or may not be true. However, we *all* have problems of varying kinds and it most definitely is not God's intent for us to pit each other's problems and experiences against one another to see who is suffering the most. Some people have the erroneous idea that evidence of *more* suffering will help others who may have less. I think it is God's purpose to have us get our eyes off of those comparisons and get them on Him and what He can do and in fact has promised to do, if we'd let Him.

What has this to do with frustrations, anyway? They are all weapons that the enemy uses to torture us into giving up, a phony promise to be free of the suffering now, to live and let live. What an ugly scheme, but how easy to be persuaded, if we take our eyes off of Jesus. In effect, what the enemy is really saying is not "be free of it," but just postpone it for a while and then you can suffer it for eternity apart from God. It is that reminder that makes me rejoice in suffering, because our Lord Jesus Christ suffered too, and paid the supreme price to free us forever. Well, I still haven't answered the question completely. First, I have stated that it is an attitude of thankfulness and joy in knowing you belong to Christ, being assured of His love, to be justified and sanctified and sealed with the Holy Spirit. In getting that understood, we step out in faith and begin to be open to His work in our lives. Now this is where I want to bring in my earlier points. As long as we focus totally on our sufferings, our growth is slowed greatly. I am guilty of this, so I know what I'm talking about. There is a tendency for each of us to be constantly "wallowing" in the suffering. Here is the old self-pity trip again. We get so caught up in all the problems that we can't get ourselves up above them where Christ would have us. It can be likened to quicksand. The more you struggle, the more you sink. What you (and I) need to do is get on solid ground. In fact, on solid rock, Jesus Christ, *the* Rock.

Yes, I know all of that, you say, but what can I actually do, outside of developing the right attitude and vision for myself? That is the second point. We step out and build His strength into our Christian experience. We begin to "mend fences" and build foundations. We try, through the work of the Holy Spirit, to lift ourselves out of the quicksand. I would like to name six important building blocks of the Christian faith that have helped me personally. I know that many of you use the same things and they are nothing new, but let's consider them a reinforcement as we look towards Him and away from the pit. Prayer and constant communication with God about *all* aspects of my life, good and bad, is the first. It is that continual open line to God for strength and understanding. Reading and studying God's Word regularly is next. We never hesitate to give our bodies food, but we often are lacking in the spiritual food that will bring new life. Thirdly, obedience to what God is saying through His Word, not the legalistic kind of law-obeying that solves nothing, but following what God would have us do, through His wonderful gift of grace. Fourth is Christian fellowship and service, with a strong and loving body of believers and with Christian friends. Isolation and aloneness will bear *no* fruit, just more agony. Fifth, being a witness to your faith by the way you act, the way you talk, the way you love, the way you forgive—and *forget*. His light shining through us every moment, even during the heaviest times. And last, recognizing that this whole thing is real and pure and beautiful and not just a big Christian "game" we are playing and coating it all with the purest and most intense *unconditional* love that you can give. And if you can't give it, then ask Him to show you how, and let Him give it through you. It is working for me and it will for you.

May God continue to pour out His blessings upon all of you and uplift you during those moments when the hurt becomes too deep.

Love in Christ,
Bob

* * *

Christmas Greetings to You All,   December 1976

This month marks the anniversary of one year of newsletters sent out to all of our friends in Christ and it gives us reason to rejoice in what God has done over the past twelve months. We are very thankful for the blessings that He has bestowed upon this ministry in the form of answered prayer and changed lives. All has not been good on the surface, as we have had many struggles, both individually and as a group. We praise Him for even those things, however, as He has turned many of them around for good and built into us additional strength. We still have so much to learn, but we are more open now as a result of our mistakes, allowing God to use even negative things to work for

His glory. It has been a fruitful year in many ways. The ministry has grown dramatically, and our newsletter outreach has doubled. In addition, correspondence from all over the world has increased markedly, and we are thankful for each one of you that has written to express your ideas or share your lives. Thank you from all of us. And we are grateful for your support and love. Our greatest hope is that the next year will be an even greater blessing as we wrestle with common problems and concerns in love and sensitivity, as God would have us do. When we are able to allow the Holy Spirit to take over, then and only then can He work the miracles that are already ours.

There are a number of times throughout the calendar year that the love of God through Jesus Christ is brought to a closer level than at other times, and it is with great joy that we experience another Advent season. No matter where we are or what we do, it is a time when we can really reflect on the true meaning of Christmas. There is much to be said about that during these times, and most churches attempt to focus on that meaning. It is so easy to get "off track" with so many commercial things going on at the same time. We have to stop and think seriously about it as we reflect upon what God made possible for all of us through the greatest single event in history. But what does Christmas mean to you? I can tell you what it means to me, but I have been sharing it over the past twelve months in one form or another, and I can sum it all up by saying I rejoice in the fact that I am a Christian and know Jesus Christ personally as my Lord. He *is* Lord, mine and yours, and it is the reason to rise above our problems and shout with joy that we have received the greatest gift of all. It thrills me beyond description, and when I hear the seasonal music playing softly in the distance, my heart beats faster. What peace, despite the pain.

Is that the true Christmas spirit? Well, it is part of it, for sure. The rest has been said in so many ways but it all adds up to the same thing, really. I especially like the way the author J.I. Packer states it in his book *Knowing God*, written a few years ago. This book is one of the finest I have ever read on God, although rather deep and scholarly. I would like to take the liberty of quoting what he has to say about the true Christmas spirit. I think it hits home and should be helpful as we look to Him more closely during this special time. Dr. Packer says, "The Christmas message is that there is hope for a ruined humanity . . . hope of pardon, hope of peace with God, hope of glory . . . because at the Father's will Jesus Christ became poor, and was born in a stable so that thirty years later He might hang on a cross. It is the most wonderful message that the world has ever heard, or will hear. . . . It ought to mean the reproducing in human lives of the temper of Him who for our sakes became poor at the first Christmas . . . for the Christmas spirit is the spirit of those who, like their Master, live their whole lives on the principle of making themselves poor . . . spending and being spent . . . to enrich their fellowmen, giving time, trouble, care and concern, to do good to others . . . and not just their own friends . . . in whatever way there seems need. There are not as many who show this spirit as there should be. If God in mercy revives us, one of the things He will do will be to work more of this spirit in our hearts and lives. If we desire spiritual quickening for ourselves individually, one step we should take is to seek to cultivate this spirit. 'Ye know the grace of our Lord Jesus Christ, that, though he was rich, yet for your sakes he became poor, that ye through his poverty might be rich' (2 Cor. 8:9 KJV).

I want to conclude this final newsletter of the year 1976 by speaking personally to all of you. First, I want to thank each one of you who has taken the time and effort to write and share a part of your life. Those letters have been the greatest blessing in this ministry and I treasure the relationship that has been created through this correspondence. My problem has increasingly been to answer all of you as promptly as I might desire, so I ask your continued patience in waiting for a reply. Please know that you are in my thoughts and prayers and that eventually you will receive a personal reply to your letter. Until God provides a full-time worker in our midst, time for everything will be at a premium. Secondly, I want to share with you the joy that I find in knowing that we are all together as a part of Christ's body and that we can look above all of our problems and see Him loving us, caring about us, and molding our lives. This was brought home to me just recently when I attended a presentation of Handel's "Messiah" by the Golden Gate Baptist Theological Seminary in Mill Valley. I have heard this work many times over the years and have even sung in a performance with the Festival Chorus while attending San Francisco State University. It never loses its meaning nor ever gets outdated. Rather, it continues to lift me up to new heights as I listen to those precious words of our Lord set to this beautiful music. During this particular performance, I sat quietly listening and pondering the past year in my mind and the joy and peace of what Christmas really means welled up in me afresh. I could feel the love filling my whole being, and I realized anew what knowing Him is all about. The words rang out so clearly, powerfully, as I sat in awe one more time. "Worthy is the Lamb that was slain, to receive power and riches and wisdom and strength and honor and glory and blessing." Of all sacred music, this one work has been more significant in my life than any other and each time I listen, it has new meaning. So, in the words of Paul, let me end by quoting 1 Corinthians 15:58. "Therefore, my beloved brethren, be steadfast, immovable, always abounding in the work of the Lord, knowing that in the Lord your labor is not in vain." Have a joyous Christmas, knowing this.

Love in Him,
Bob

* * *

Those interested in the ministry of Love in Action or who wish to receive our newsletter or any of our available cassette tapes can contact us at the following address:

Love in Action
2130 Fourth Street
San Rafael, California 94901
Telephone: 415-457-9489